MUSIC MAKER

An appreciation of the life and work of

Clifford Harker

This book is dedicated to all those who have valued the life and example of Clifford Harker, and especially dedicated to those many people who have willingly and enthusiastically contributed towards the making of this book.

MUSIC MAKER

An appreciation of the life and work of

CLIFFORD HARKER

Margaret Hilton

Verona House Publications

Published by Verona House Publications,
(J.B. and M.E. Hilton), 382 Church Road,
Frampton Cotterell, Bristol, BS36 2AB,
England

Copyright © Margaret Hilton, 2001

British Library Cataloguing in Publication Data
A catalogue record for this book is available from the British Library

ISBN 0 952 5015 2 X

Typeset in 10/12pt Times New Roman by
John Hilton

Printed in Great Britain by
Bookcraft Limited,
Midsomer Norton,
Bath BA3 4BS

CONTENTS

List of Illustrations   *vii*

Preface   *ix*

1. Salvete – The Music Maker   1
2. Paths Untrod   18
3. Bristol   45
4. Choirs, orchestras, soloists   78
5. Churches, organs, recitals   117
6. Compositions and arrangements   142
7. Leisure activities – the lighter side   148
8. In retirement and Valete   155

Appendix I   Clifford and Composition   *xi*

Appendix II   Table of major works performed   *xiii*

Acknowledgements   *xx*

LIST OF ILLUSTRATIONS

		Page
1.	Clifford Harker	Frontispiece
2.	Newcastle Cathedral Choir and officials, 1938	4
3.	Alick Maclean, conductor of the Spa Orchestra, Scarborough, 1935	7
4.	Programme of music for the Spa, Scarborough, 1935	7
5.	Alwyn Surplice	10
6.	British Forces desert camp about 20 miles from Cairo	20
7.	Cairo Cathedral floodlit for V.E. Night	20
8.	Bishop Llewellyn Gwynne	22
9.	Archdeacon Francis Johnston	22
10.	Rev. Arthur Burrell	22
11.	Relaxing on the Cathedral Steps	22
12.	Chareh Maarouf – 'Music for All' sign	24
13.	A La Groppi Restaurant in 'Music for All' Centre	24
14.	The North Garden at 'Music for All'	24
15.	'Music for All' concert	27
16.	Front of 'Messiah' programme	28
17.	Men's Choral Society rehearsal	30
18.	Choral rehearsal in Cairo Cathedral	30
19.	Press photograph in the Report of 'Messiah' performance	32
20.	Arthur Reckless	33
21.	Sketch of you know who (unsigned).	35
22.	Cairo Cathedral Choir, 1942	44
23.	Clifford and his 'boys'	58
24.	Bristol Cathedral Choir – Clifford conducting	72
25.	Bristol Cathedral Special Choir rehearsal in the Colston Hall, Bristol, with the Bournmouth Symphony Orchestra, November, 1957	91
26.	Bristol Choral Society 'Messiah' in Colston Hall, Bristol, December, 1987	105
27.	The Lord Mayor's Chapel Choir	111
28.	St. George's Church, Jesmond, Newcastle, Interior	118
29.	Newcastle Cathedral organ	121
30.	Cairo Cathedral, Exterior	128
31.	Cairo Cathedral, Interior	128
32.	The organ of Cairo Cathedral	128

33. St. Andrew's Church, Rugby — 130
34. Bristol Cathedral. Rear and garden — 132
35. Bristol Cathedral. Nave — 132
36. Bristol Cathedral. Organ case and choir — 134
37. Bristol Cathedral. Eastern Lady Chapel organ — 134
38. C. H. at the organ of Bristol Cathedral — 136
39. The Lord Mayor's Chapel, College Green, Bristol — 138
40. First page of Iste Confessor — 144
41. Part of manuscript arrangement by C.H. for Distant Trumpet (Verdi: Requiem) — 147
42. The Cathedral garden, showing the headstone of Walford Davies, 1869-1941 — 160
43. Clifford's conducting batons in a case made for Him by Michael Dyer — 162

PREFACE

I felt it a great privilege to have been involved in research regarding aspects of Clifford Harker's life; the deeper I delved the more evident it became that he was admired and respected for his own self, and for the profound and lasting influence he had upon those with whom he worked.

My own contact was principally through Bristol Choral Society, of which I was a member for twenty-four years, my husband, John, exceeding that period by three years - during which time we both held various offices, getting to know Clifford a little more intimately during our period as joint Secretaries.

We all held Clifford a little in awe; not because he made himself in any way superior but because we realised his vast musical capabilities and stalwart personal principles. Yet, he spoke in such a way which seemed to indicate he considered you knew as much as he did about it all (not always the case, by far), and we knew that he expected of others the same high standards that he set for himself. We received the incomparable and irreplaceable experience of performing a large number of the great musical works.

His performances were prepared with fine technical precision combined with perfect artistic interpretation which he desired from both singers and orchestra, and we tried to work with the same aims of perfection to ensure that both musical and administrative preparation for any concert was as he wished. Clifford's whole life had been so full, so completely absorbed in the making of music, imparting a greater love and appreciation of it upon all he encountered in his work, with a colossal amount of wisdom and dexterity acquired over the years.

Several years ago Clifford declined my request to create this book, saying "Nothing interesting". Even so, during that sad, yet somehow joyous, funeral service, when we were bidding farewell to that revered gentleman, I knew this must all be written down, and maybe this is a better time.

Many people had been familiar with some aspects of Clifford's experiences and work, yet knew nothing of how it all developed and gave us the man we knew. Clifford was always most sensitive about publicity. He did not seek overt fame yet, conversely, he naturally and rightly wanted due acknowledgement of his efforts. Those looking for sensationalism must needs look elsewhere, for these pages do not show a man of melodrama, of grandiosity and showy ostentation, but a dignified, humble servant of his profession. Idle pomp, bravado and parade were not his pretence, but a quiet panache, indicating the mind of a genius absorbed in his chosen medium - the interpretation of the music and the serving of the God whom he adored.

During Clifford's Bristol years his involvement with so many different sectors would make it difficult to retain clear continuity of text; thus, in order to give each aspect its proper due I have set out, in the first instance, a chronological account of his life, then developed various aspects in greater detail in subsequent chapters, thus avoiding a multiplicity of interwoven activities which took place during the same period.

Chapter sub-headings

It was in 1912 that the fifty-five year old Edward Elgar was working hard in his home (Severn House, Hampstead, London) to complete his newest composition 'The Music Makers'. Clifford Harker was born that year, too, and was to develop a deep love of all Elgar's music, and to champion that music throughout his own life.

It was observed, by many people, that if one composer had influenced Clifford more than any, it was undoubtedly Elgar. I feel there was a sure affinity between the two musicians, whose lives overlapped during an age when many musicians of vision felt that their responsibility was a mission to 'renew the world as of yore'. This vision is also reflected by such composers as Ralph Vaughan Williams in his setting of Walt Whitman's poem 'Towards the Unknown Region', and Hubert Parry's musical setting of his own poem 'A Vision of Life'.

Edward Elgar was inspired by Arthur O'Shaughnessy's Ode 'The Music Makers', and musically portrayed the highest human aspiration. He deliberately used musical quotations from the whole range of his past compositions and as the work progressed the best ideas of his whole maturity passed in succession - Enigma (which dominated the whole), Gerontius, Sea Pictures, and the two symphonies, with strains of The Apostles and the Violin Concerto. When one remembers Clifford Harker , he is seen as a serious musician who certainly possessed great sensitivity in all that he did, thus imparting his own vision of life with all its music. It is for this reason that I have prefaced each chapter with a quotation from 'The Music Makers'.

Everyone has their story - this has been told simply and straightforward from the inside by many willing contributors who have enjoyed the challenge of learning the greatest musical works of all time, including many by Clifford himself; knowing the problems posed by some pieces, rehearsing sometimes under difficult conditions, but who have felt excitement and exhilaration of taking part in something memorable.

Well, readers, you may judge for yourselves if it has been "nothing interesting".........

M.H.
November, 2001

CHAPTER 1
SALVETE - THE MUSIC MAKER
'One man with a dream shall go forth and conquer a crown'.

In the gathering twilight of a January afternoon, the Cathedral Church of the Holy and Undivided Trinity in Bristol was packed to capacity with people, young and old, who had met together for one purpose - to bid farewell to a remarkable and saintly gentleman. Choral Evensong was to be sung in thanksgiving to God for the life of **Clifford Harker**, former Organist and Master of the Choristers of that Cathedral, and a man of great ability. He had been resident in Bristol for fifty years; he had loved every stone of the Cathedral; now hundreds were gathered there to bid a fond and grateful farewell.

But this is the culmination of a life's journey; what follows will reveal a pilgrimage used very much to the full; a life completely absorbed, from beginning to end, and dedicated to two things - a total love of music and a commitment to the service of the God whom he worshipped with his whole heart.

Arthur Clifford Harker's life began in Newcastle upon Tyne on 5th February, 1912. He was fortunate to have been born of such parents for **Arthur** and **Elizabeth Harker** provided him with an ideal and loving family environment and were naturally delighted when their firstborn began to show musical talent at an early age. Arthur Harker was well-known locally, not only for his own musical interests, but he worked as Music critic for the Newcastle Evening Chronicle under the pseudonym 'Counterpoint'. He was respected for his shrewd and careful reporting of local musical events and reviews of recent gramophone recordings, of which there was an increasing abundance as more advanced techniques in recording methods made the gramophone available to more and more people. The Harker household would constantly resound with tunes coming from the 'wireless' and the family gramophone, on which Arthur played many new recordings sent to him by the record companies. The young Clifford was surrounded by wonderful sounds of the Great Masters, and this was one of the means whereby his love of music was awakened and developed into his own youthful efforts as he strove to master keyboard skills and all rudimentary knowledge of musical notation.

Encouraged by his parents, who were undoubtedly a great influence in Clifford's formative years as a musician, he progressed quickly and it soon became apparent that he had much musical ability.

However, despite the abundance of gramophone records which regularly arrived at the house for review, Arthur Harker never allowed his son to listen to them until he had first learned the works by playing them as piano duets. This may have been a frustrating practice for any ordinary boy, but for Clifford it served to give him a profound knowledge of a vast number of great orchestral works such as the Beethoven and Brahms symphonies, and this disciplined mode of learning became his own advocate for life and one which he always encouraged in his own pupils. To begin with the score, and not someone else's interpretation of it, enabled Clifford, all his life, to read and even hear the music in his head as he prepared a work for performance. Perhaps he was born with a natural perception but, it is certain, the discipline of working with a score before hearing the music played was a wonderful aid to the development of techniques which were to expand with experience and application. It must certainly be true that following the effort involved in learning the score, the experience of hearing the sounds realised by orchestral instruments would be most thrilling and in consequence give an early appreciation of the make-up of orchestral consummation.

Clifford received an excellent general education at **Dame Alleyn's Grammar School in Newcastle**. There was a chance to become a chorister at **Newcastle Cathedral** but it never came about and, although he was in the choir at his own church, maybe it was just as well, as singing was never his best attribute (as anyone who heard him as an adult would readily confirm). Nevertheless, his musical abilities were recognised and he played his first church service at the tender age of nine years.

At the age of fourteen Clifford felt his first pangs of grief when his dearly loved mother, herself still quite young, died of cancer, leaving an all-male household of father, Clifford and his younger brother, **Geoffrey**. It goes without saying that loss of wife and mother made it difficult to bear in a family so close-knit, but life had to go on for Arthur, despite his grief, and bravely he undertook the roles of both father and mother to his two growing boys: Clifford - quiet and studious, and Geoffrey - always a dashing and extrovert sportsman and adored by his brother.

The family lived at 58 Coniston Avenue, West Jesmond, but some time before 1937 moved to 4 Cavendish Place, Jesmond.

Arthur Harker and his boys were closely connected with **St. George's Church**, in **Jesmond, Newcastle upon Tyne**, where they worshipped regularly. Clifford served his apprenticeship there in the church choir, along with other boys whom he had known since boyhood - **John Shield, John Dunn, John Moreland, Leonard Kerr** - and learned choral expertise under the revered **Dr. J.E.Hutchinson, F.R.C.O.** Dr. Hutchinson played an important part in Clifford's musical development and experience in choral performance, as he greatly admired both organ and conducting styles of his mentor. The boys in that choir had great and happy times together and Clifford began to conduct choirs and orchestras from the age of about seventeen, and at only nineteen he gave his first full performance of Messiah with orchestra. Only a year later he was to conduct several orchestral performances of his own compositions and had a number of polished compositions already in publication. Many of Clifford's young friends followed his career with keen interest long after he had left Newcastle.

Another friend, **Edward Fairley** (who took over the Cathedral choir after Clifford left for war service), along with **Tom Cleverly** and **Harry**

Hoult, often recalled the great days of their choral singing in Newcastle long after Bristol had 'taken Clifford to its heart' and often jokingly reminded him that fine musicians, as well as coal, came from Newcastle! Edward Fairley and Clifford were very close friends, especially on the subject of choir training. Clifford was greatly appreciated and loved at the Cathedral and was always regarded as 'always a pleasure to be with and a real Christian gentleman'. Clifford always remained a true son of that city. During Clifford's career they progressed with their own musical interests, some remaining in the Jesmond church choir for a lifetime's singing, and received news of Clifford from soloists and instrumentalists visiting the far north, getting glowing reports of his work in Bristol. On his occasional visits to Newcastle, especially after his retirement, he often attended Matins at the Cathedral and met again with former friends.

A particular friend from that era was **John Healey** who, like Clifford, was seriously intent on a career in music. At John Healey's home Clifford spent many an enjoyable hour making music with his friend - playing piano duets, mostly of the Haydn symphonies - all this remembered with great affection as each followed his own career path. Together they progressed in their studies and by 1930 both were highly respected musicians in Newcastle circles. In fact, they both felt 'on line' for the post of assistant to the Cathedral Organist, **Dr. William Ellis**. Healey recalled how Clifford "carried it off - probably because he was taller and better-looking - with his usual panache". In the event, Clifford took over the duties at **Newcastle Cathedral** and, although still in his early twenties became Organist when Dr. Ellis retired through illness, carrying out his responsibilities with supreme confidence. He approached the work with professionalism from the beginning which in all probability reflected in some part, his father's ideals of perfection along with his own deep desire that only his best was acceptable both to himself and others, most of all the God he had come to love and depend on. **Mr. Bill Stafford**, who joined the Cathedral choir at the age of eight in 1938, remembered hearing a discussion between two young boys which ran as follows:

    1st. boy: I think Mr. Harker is a better organist than Dr. Ellis.
    2nd. boy: He can't be because Dr. Ellis is a Dr.
    1st. boy: Well, when Mr. Harker is a Dr. he will still be better than Dr. Ellis.

Word of this reached Dr. Ellis!

Clifford was making the organ his chosen instrument and he loved every moment playing the mighty beast, especially for church services but, in
addition, he needed complementary fulfilment, having a vast amount of physical energy in addition to an unbounded enthusiasm for his work. Thus, he gained experience in his youth by accompanying (and sometimes conducting) local choirs who were keen to encourage his obvious talent. One

Newcastle Cathedral Choir 1938
Clifford Harker – Deputy Organist, 2nd row, 7th from right.
Dr. William Ellis (Master of the Music) 2nd row, 9th from right.

such choir was the **Newcastle Bach Choir**, the Director of which was **William Gillies Whittaker**. All this gave Clifford invaluable preparation and experience which carried him through to the eventual appointments in which he was to conduct and direct substantial choral works with large-scale choirs. As he approached a more mature career the work of training choristers and choirs would be his forte and this early chance to conduct helped him to advance into greater things with both feet firmly on the ground.

For his professional training Clifford entered the **Royal College of Organists** in June, 1931, passing Associateship in January, 1932, and Fellowship in July, 1933. He entered the **Royal College of Music** in 1934 and studied under distinguished teachers: piano with **Marmaduke Barton**, organ with **Dr.Henry Ley**, conducting with **Malcolm Sargent** and composition with **Ralph Vaughan Williams**. Receiving this first class tutoring meant that his natural talents were developed to the full and these wise mentors were to have a lasting influence upon his musical life. He was awarded the ARCM in December, 1934, and the La Fontaine Prize for Solo Piano. He continued studies during 1935. Studying in London, with the 'greats' (in addition to his admiration of conductors like **Beecham** and **Barbirolli**) served to complement skills already learned from his youthful idol, Dr. Hutchinson who, doubtless, encouraged Clifford in his earnest aspirations.

Barbirolli, incidentally, strongly believed that conductors were born, not made, and always refused to teach conducting for that reason. He asserted that people could teach technique for ever but, ultimately, the conductor must study the score, get it all into his head, then translate all the 'feeling' through his arm. (One wonders if what his mother thought was her lovely baby happily waving his chubby little arms in response to her lullabies was really Clifford getting started........)

During this period, another conductor was to make a profound impression upon Clifford's musical development. This was **Alick Maclean**, conductor of the **Spa Orchestra** in **Scarborough**. Maclean became extremely well known in the north eastern part of Britain and was a distinguished and popular gentleman. To Clifford he was the 'cat's whiskers', and Clifford found in his conducting everything that was to be desired by way of sensitive interpretation of all he performed. He felt Maclean had the ability to make a trifling serenade sound enchanting.

In those days, the popular 36-strong Spa Orchestra provided music in the delightful setting of the Spa Palm Court every morning at 11 o'clock and every evening at 8 o'clock throughout the summer season at this attractive and popular seaside resort. The orchestra played good quality music of all the best composers, not only the lighter pieces of composers such as Johann Strauss, Sullivan, Noel Coward, Franz Lehar, Albert Ketèlby and Eric Coates but, equally, played works by the musical 'giants' - Bach, Tchaikovsky, Bellini, Holst, Puccini and Ravel. Residents and holidaymakers alike were treated to a veritable feast of good, superbly played , musical concerts. In contrast to today's highly priced concerts, in 1935 it was possible to enjoy a series of fourteen concerts for a mere six shillings.

Clifford took every opportunity to bask in the luxury of this feature during the summer, eventually making himself known to the man he so admired.

With a number of short compositions already completed (and handy in his pocket) Clifford approached Alick Maclean and found him interested, for the standard of writing was very good. This resulted in his orchestral piece 'Meditation' receiving its first performance on 28th June, 1935, at the Spa in Scarborough and, even more thrilling, the twenty-three year old Clifford was invited to conduct his own music. It was a great and proud moment for the Harker family! Other items in the programme were Holst's St. Paul's Suite for string orchestra, Schubert's Symphony No. 5 in B flat and Rimsky-Korsakov's 'Capriccio Espagnol'.

Alick Maclean's style of conducting influenced Clifford's as much as anyone's, for whilst Sargent conveyed professional techniques, people like Maclean exuded the style and charisma for which Clifford himself became admired throughout his subsequent career.

Whilst studying in London the wise counsel of Ralph Vaughan Williams' compositional tutoring was an invaluable aid as Clifford developed his own writing style. In fact, when complimented on a piece of his own writing, Clifford would casually remark "Oh, it's just a piece of bad Vaughan Williams, you know". Such was Clifford's self-effacement, but it showed a real appreciation of the music of this great composer, and a striving to achieve comparable compositional skills. Later on, (or perhaps even earlier on) Clifford began to develop a real appreciation of, and affinity to, the music of **Edward Elgar**. These two very 'English' style composers were to influence Clifford's output in performance as well as writing techniques, and their music was to feature largely in his concert programmes and choice of music for cathedral worship.

On completing his studies at the Royal College of Music, which awarded him a First Prize for his A.R.C.O. Diploma, further studies brought him F.R.C.O. whilst still in his early twenties.

With formal training behind him, Clifford could now contemplate a properly qualified career in music which, for him, meant the return to his beloved Newcastle and family, where he became sub-Organist of **St. Nicholas' Cathedral** and Organist and Choirmaster of **St. Andrew's Parish Church**.

When the Vicar and Provost of the Cathedral (Rev. John Champain) retired he felt so appreciative of Clifford's work that he wrote a glowing testimonial. The following is an extract:

> '.... I want to put on paper a record of my gratitude to him for the services he has given and for the spirit in which he has given them He is of course an accomplished and outstanding executant of the organ - others can testify to this who have more claim to speak about

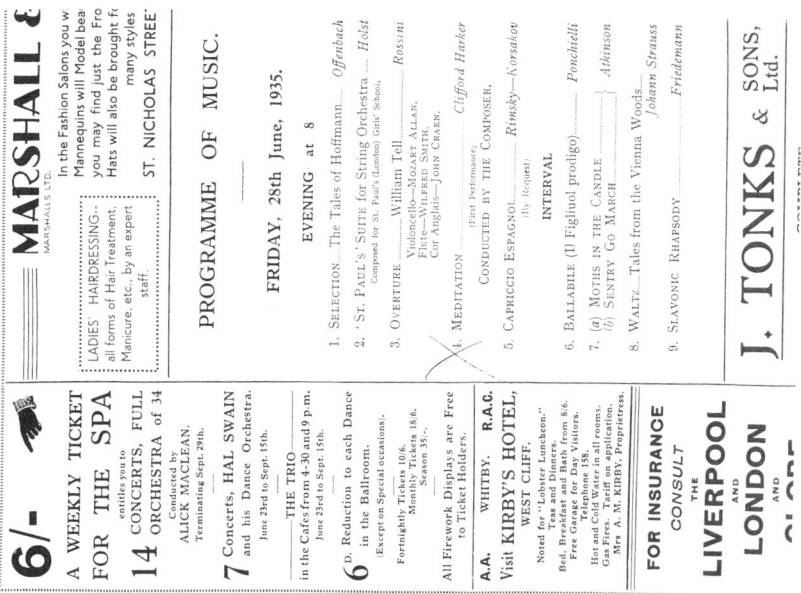

3. Alick Maclean, conductor of the Spa Orchestra, Scarborough, 1935
4. Programme of Music for the Spa, Scarborough, 1935

this side of his work. I have to say that it has made a great difference to us to have him about the Cathedral. He has the spirit of real devotion which becomes infectious through his playing. He has the power of making people want to sing and worship. That is really important and I have been much struck how much this power is in such a young man. He is himself an excellent character with an attractive personality. I believe any church or cathedral will be most fortunate to obtain his services when his time comes to leave Newcastle'

    (signed) John Champain,
    Vicar of Newcastle   Feb. 19, 1938

Already his devotional personality was having an effect where it mattered most.

So far, everything seems to portray Clifford as a serious-minded and completely strait-laced young man. True, he had been single minded and worked hard to be worthy of the position of responsibility in which he now found himself. But it would be far from the truth to portray him as wholly serious. He was, indeed, as lively and fun loving as the next person. Nevertheless, he was a young man with a few chosen friends of like mind, rather than being 'one of the boys', surrounded by a crowd of jokers. This was Clifford's personality and he got on well with his friends and colleagues, enjoying their company and humour like the intelligent person he was. He was never lonely, although he spent much of his time living alone, because he always had the company of his music and the ability to indulge in his life's passion whenever he wished - with or without others.

Somewhere along the line Clifford developed a keen interest in lighter music. It was, in fact, all around him. His was the era of keen operatic societies and the music of Gilbert and Sullivan, Lionel Monckton, Edward German, and the like, whose witty scripts and lively, attractive tunes gave pleasure to so many people. It also attracted Clifford's appreciation and sense of humour (which he had in abundance) and delectation. It is said that, as a young man he knew every word of the **Gilbert and Sullivan** operas as well as all the music. Yes, our Clifford was as keen as anyone on the 'pops' of the day, thoroughly enjoying the local performances and, more than likely, playing the tunes for his own and others' enjoyment and entertainment.

Later on he was to give this enjoyment to some of his choirs, realising how 'jolly' this music was and that they, too, needed 'something light' now and then. He thoroughly enjoyed giving concert performances of a number of light operas.

With the prospect of a fulfilling and productive continuing of his chosen career, Clifford Harker settled down like so many of his friends and contemporaries, and it may be that he would have remained the sole benison of the North for his lifetime, were it not for the hand of Fate which intervened and interrupted this idyllic scene, in the monstrous form of the Second World War. Clifford's own recollections of the 1914-18 war would be few, being still very young when that war came to an end but it was more than likely that, as the aftermath continued for a number of years, he would be reminded again and again of the horrors of the battlefield by observing people returning to civilian life, and everyone attempting to rebuild their lives. Gradually, in Britain, normality was restored, though on the Continent the uneasy political situation continued the mouldering which, in 1939, culminated in a flare-up and the start of hostilities once more.

There were surely many times during the Second World War years when Clifford reflected on the seeming idyllic life he had come to know as he revelled in the many activities he had set for himself. He was doing exactly what he had planned for his life and career and, as a convinced Christian, he believed he was serving God in all that he undertook.

Despite a busy schedule there was even time to compose and he had begun studies for a Bachelor of Music degree. A life of music had seemed full of promise; now all Clifford could do was to await call-up in the service of his country.

Both brothers were eligible for military service and both passed all tests and health requirements. It was a great adventure for the gregarious Geoffrey, who entered the Royal Air Force and became a navigator. Clifford, following his adored brother's choice volunteered for the **RAF** and was told he would be trained as a wireless operator. The tedious business of 'square bashing' and initial training, some of which took him to the Shetland Isles, seemed quite out of character for Clifford and although he was not the only airman to feel like a fish out of water, necessity enabled him to bear all with a noble spirit and he tried hard to get it all right. Perhaps the rhythm which gradually came with marching up and down the parade ground became second nature but when it came to being confronted with 'bally machines', technical operations got in the way of his sensitive fingers and it was all he could do to pass the tests to qualify him for his new job.

Throughout his life Clifford could never get to grips with things mechanical and even when riding a bicycle every time was like a first time and it was all too easy to ride straight into a brick wall! But - he always did his best, however difficult the task, and it was with enormous pains that he carried out his R.A.F. duties, dubbing himself 'the world's worst radio operator' - and bore it all with great dignity.

Whilst on a marching exercise in Blackpool Clifford met **Alwyn Surplice**, one of two men who were a great support to him during the war years. One said to the other "I've got to be careful with my feet, I'm an organist, you know". As the war continued the two men were brought together from time to time and became great friends. Even when service days were ended Clifford enjoyed a long friendship with Alwyn and his wife, Mollie. When Alwyn became assistant to **Sir William Harris** at Windsor, Clifford succeeded him at **Bristol** Cathedral.

5. Alwyn Surplice

Although he did not know it then, good times were just around the corner for Clifford as in 1941 he found himself posted to the **Middle East**. He embarked on a troopship bound for **Egypt**, where he was destined to stay for the remainder of his service life.

Maybe Clifford found some music-making in his early days as an aircraftman, he certainly never overlooked any opportunity to make use of his talents. Making music was his first instinct and he lost no time in gathering together interested men aboard the converted **Liner 'Samaria'**, encouraging them to sing away their boredom.

As the ship laboriously made its way to the Canal Zone it was essential to go by a very roundabout route. Subtle and devious tactics were necessary for the troopship to remain undetected by enemy submarines lurking deep down in the waters. Troopships were always escorted by destroyers for a large part of the journey, the boats sailing round the north coast of Ireland, far out into the Atlantic Sea before turning south to skirt the western coast of Africa, where the first port of call would be **Sierra Leone** (then a British colony) for fuel, water and supplies. Then it would be on to **Cape Town**, **Durban**, and a final dash to the **Suez** port, having successfully manoeuvred the eastern coast of Africa with the protection of South African destroyers. Some journey - of three months' duration! Also long and tedious for those on board, and in non-too-luxurious conditions. When the ship reached the tropics there was the physical adjustment to unaccustomed heat in addition to all the trials of war.

The daily routine on a troopship was fairly similar - after breakfast there was 'boat parade' when each unit, having their own deck, would report to their own allotted lifeboat, don lifejackets, and perform a necessary and regular drill until it became second nature for a speedy evacuation of the ship in emergency. Every inch of the ship would be used to advantage, even the luggage hold was converted to quarters and hammocks were fixed on hooks for the men, whilst officers occupied the few cabins available. Clifford found conditions were 'frightful' and, by all accounts, he had to spend every night of the three months sleeping on the bar floor. A makeshift chapel was set up where the Chaplain would hold Sunday services and be available for discussion and advice on matters spiritual. There were opportunities for deck games for those with energy and plenty of chances of playing cards or other activities within the limited space of an overcrowded vessel. Letters home were written on an aerogramme, limiting the length of words and, of course, heavily censored. These messages were put on microfilm, relayed back home, and rewritten when they reached Britain, to be delivered to the recipient in an almost identical form.

On this particular troopship things were to turn out a little different; the six weeks aboard ship, despite its frustrations, did not keep Clifford Harker idle. He sensed an opportunity - here were hundreds of servicemen with nothing much to occupy them for most of the time - so, somehow, he set about finding entertainment for them - musical entertainment! Neither did the absence of printed copies deter him. He set about writing songs from memory, adding his own arrangements (some of the very first 'Arr. C.H.' perhaps?) and ruling his own manuscript paper. With typical enthusiasm he rallied his own troops and found much interest; they sang well, and he formed the ship's choral society which soon became a popular feature during the voyage. When the boat docked at **Durban** it soon became known that amongst these troops there was a thriving group of singers and so the choral society of fifty men was invited to give a concert in the Garrison Theatre at the City Hall. The date - 8th July, 1941. The Durban newspaper recorded the event:

Superb Soldiers' Choir

No doubt many radio listeners and those of the public who managed to squeeze into Garrison Theatre in the City Hall on Sunday night share my admiration for the soldiers' choir of 50 which has been performing over the weekend. The inspiration of this superb choir is Clifford Harker, Doctor of Music, and now a very humble unit in the R.A.F. Most of the choristers have had a cathedral choir experience, but before Harker moulded them into shape they had never sung together before. The result of his work is a choir which compares with some of the best that have come out of choir-singing Wales ......

Clifford had written out folk songs, sea shanties, student songs and some church music - all from memory - which were so well performed aboard ship that the choir was fully confident (as was their conductor) in broadcasting three programmes in two days. In addition to concerts, Clifford led the choir in two sung services every Sunday morning.

It had been Clifford's good fortune to meet **Roger Wilson**, a church organist from London, during the voyage, and the two men forged a strong partnership, combining their musical gifts to train the men's choir on board and to entertain the troops during the long voyage. Roger also helped to provide the music of the Cathedral in Cairo, acted as accompanist to the Services Choral Society and gave recitals in both Cathedral and Music for All programmes.

When the 'Samaria' finally reached the Port of Suez the troops were despatched to their various units and it seemed that the choral society would become just a memory. However, Clifford's fame had already been noted and as he arrived at his delegated posting, **Cairo**, he found that **Group Captain T.H.Evans** was seriously intending to make use of his outstanding talents and, in no time, Clifford found himself seconded from R.A.F. duties to run **'Music for All'**, a centre for culture, comfort and entertainment for the forces in Cairo and surrounding area.

The centre had opened several years earlier and was sponsored by **Lady Dorothea Russell Pasha** a resident in Cairo. It had become a calm oasis in a war-torn world.

So it happened that September, 1941, began a period which, despite the war with all its restrictions and uncertainties, became one of the most exhilarating and rewarding parts of Clifford's career, lasting until the war's ending brought eventual return to England shortly after September, 1945.

Cairo newspapers were regularly full of praise for Clifford's music and leadership and inspirational playing after he was appointed organist at **All Saints' Cathedral, Cairo**.

Another wartime comrade and close friend who was able to give Clifford much support during the war was **John Bennett** of **Northampton**, whose lively spirit provided Clifford with encouragement as well as appreciation of his work in Cairo. An amateur viola player, John played in Clifford's Cairo orchestras and continued to do so occasionally in his post-war orchestras.

Sights set to greater things for the future and, with an extremely busy and absorbing schedule which occupied most of his thoughts and hours, Clifford still found time to pursue his own education. He continued music studies by correspondence, written work being sent back and forth to **Dr. Ben Burrows** as he worked for an external B.Mus. which was awarded by Durham University upon his return to England.

Clifford's period in Egypt was utterly pleasurable for him and he revelled in making music, running two concerts a day, seven days a week, for over four years, in addition to duties at the Cathedral. He performed some of the great choral works, including Handel's Messiah, as well as several operas and programmes of light music with his two choirs - a male voice choir comprising many of the singers who had joined aboard ship, and a ladies choir of servicewomen and ladies resident in Cairo. The programmes gave a great deal of respite and pleasure to thousands of people who were in Cairo, or passing through, and he was constantly receiving accolade after accolade for his work.

Despite personal triumph, Clifford never lost sight of purpose. He was able to do not only the thing he enjoyed but he was able to impart an immense amount of pleasure to people who were really fighting the war and he was very conscious of the fact that this was <u>his</u> opportunity to serve, to help to revive and renew wounded or shattered lives, to encourage others in their determination to fight for what was right as they came to Cairo and went on again.

But Clifford had to endure personal sorrow alongside it all. His dearly loved father died (of natural causes) and his adored brother, Geoffrey, was killed in action over France in 1944. For Clifford, now alone in the world, the loss was hard to bear and the prospect of returning to England, notwithstanding the ending of hostilities, was not a consolation nor attractive to him. He had become regarded with great affection in his work, both at the Music For All Centre and at the Cathedral where the saintly **Bishop Gwynne**, knowing of Clifford's bereavement, and with genuine Christian love and concern, took the young man and gently consoled and supported him in his time of grieving, as did many Cathedral folk. At the same time, Clifford's staunch faith helped him to accept his situation and to go forward with courage. As he prepared to leave Cairo he was very conscious of the thoughts and prayers of the faithful there, and was sufficed.

Fuller details of Clifford's sojourn in the Middle East are recorded in Chapter 2.

Return to post-war England was approached with a certain amount of apprehension. This was the natural reaction felt by many people who had served their country abroad in the upheaval of wartime conditions. The time had been one of trauma for many, and settling down was not easy. True, most returned to home and family, to the longed-for familiar and well-loved places, but life was different. Evidence of bombing was everywhere, people had been shocked or maimed, food was short, work was uncertain and even ten years on still saw the country still struggling to put the past behind and working for a better life. Life could never be the same as it was before 1939 - a similar situation to the aftermath of the First World War, and only gradually were people able to reshape their own lives and provide a more gratifying existence for the next generation.

So it was to a land in the throes of 'change' into which the now 34 year-old Clifford Harker returned. Doubtless he visited relatives and well-loved friends and dear familiar places, but he never settled in Newcastle after demobilisation. Instead, he was tempted to roam further south and, late in 1945, became organist of **St. Andrew's Parish Church** in **Rugby.** He also taught Music at the local **Lawrence Sherriff Grammar School** and travelled to London on several days each week to teach piano at **Trinity College.**

As Clifford departed Rugby Church, the School and the Choral Society, he left behind a goodly number of people who had themselves become enthused with a love and understanding of music and who would continue to explore and appreciate this medium for the rest of their lives.

Once again, Clifford had left his mark!

It became **Bristol's** turn to take to itself the now 37 year-old musician as, in 1949, he was appointed Organist and Master of the Choristers at the **Cathedral Church of the Holy and Undivided Trinity**, on College Green. He could not have had any notion at the time that it would be a post to be held for 34 years and, in that time, to influence the lives of countless people by his example and dedication. For many, from him they would learn professionalism, the ability to work as a team, and a duty to give of their very best - all in addition to learning the very highest of skills in singing standards and technique. To others, he taught them, in addition, to understand and interpret the music which he inspired them to love, by his own inspiration and example as a musician, and as a true Christian gentleman.

After taking up residence in Bristol Clifford undertook the directing of a number of choirs - he conducted the **Bristol Madrigal Society** for a time and, subsequently, in 1953 formed the **Cathedral Special Choir** which soon grew to number around 290 singers. The Choir performed three times a year in the Cathedral and was his great pleasure for thirty years. In 1960 he became Conductor of **Bristol Choral Society**, an equally large choir which gave three or four performances a year in the Colston Hall - an association which lasted twenty-nine years. **Bath Choral Society** also came under his baton in 1963 for twenty-four years. All these choirs performed with full orchestra drawn from professional musicians, mainly from Bristol and the West Country, but some travelled from London for the concerts, with their brief pre-concert rehearsals.

Much can be related about all Clifford's activities during this very full period of his life, and succeeding chapters will set out each aspect in greater detail.

After retirement from Bristol Cathedral, and the Special Choir, Clifford was invited to become Organist at the **Lord Mayor's Chapel** on College Green. He held this post for twelve years, playing for services on Sunday mornings throughout the year and directing the regular choir of eight voices, rendering magnificent service to that unique place of worship. Details of his time at the Lord Mayor's Chapel are also recorded in further chapters of this volume.

Throughout his life Clifford remained a bachelor and, having no family, found accommodation to suit his needs. After the war he lived for many years, both in Rugby and Bristol, in a hotel room, surrounded by a few personal effects and enjoying an independent lifestyle. He stayed for a long time in a hotel in Pembroke Road, Clifton, Bristol and, as he never owned a car, was often to be seen after Evensong waiting for a bus at the bottom of Park Street.

Moving to a flat in Codrington Place, Clifton, and later to Vyvyan Terrace gave the advantage of larger surroundings and the luxury of keeping his own Bechstein piano which he had previously housed in his room at the Cathedral.

Clifford never wanted for friends as, despite being completely absorbed in his music, he enjoyed company, and there were many loyal friends for companionship and also those who were glad to transport him to rehearsals and concerts. His close friends, realising always that he was likely to be alone at holiday times, particularly at Christmas, would extend a warm welcome to him at their home. Whilst fiercely independent, he was gracious in his praise of those who gave him help and support, particularly in his latter years.

There was, too, a great sense of humour, but it was a gentle self-deprecating one. His friend, **John Jenkins**, said that it was more instinctive for him to tell a joke against himself than to score at others' expense, and he was full of great warmth and jollity when in the company of friends. One particularly good story about himself was told of the time when he was dancing with his godmother in the ballroom of a Scandinavian cruise ship. Noting that the floor had emptied to leave only the two of them in action,

Clifford was later to discover that they had, in fact, been tango-ing to the Danish National Anthem as the ship neared Copenhagen. Choristers could rely on him for a repertoire of three innocent jokes; how do you make a Venetian blind? How do you make a Swiss roll? and (in more risqué moments) - Why did the submarine blush? In rehearsal, there were occasionally times when patience would snap but the admonishment would be sharp and short, always short-lived, and quickly he would regain good humour and illustrate his complaint with a trite remark or story.

One cannot imagine Clifford as a 'family man', yet he was genuinely fond of children - had it not been so he would never have spent so many years of his life with choristers. He was proud of his choristers, they were his musical 'sons' and (on his own admission) it was the choristers he missed most when he came to the end of his service to the Cathedral.

August was the month when Clifford took his annual holiday, when he knew his Assistant would appreciate having full rein at the Cathedral organ, and the choristers were themselves on holiday. There were many places he liked to visit on holiday at different times and some of them will be recalled in later chapters, but they were known to be working holidays for Clifford, returning refreshed and ready to take up the next year's commitments, would never fail to have completed plans for the season - works to be performed, soloists booked, and everything 'shipshape and Bristol fashion'.

For holidaying, Clifford enjoyed 'style' - one of elegance and quality. One of his favourite destinations was Scarborough with its many happy memories of his youth. He also enjoyed Bournemouth, Sidmouth, Nice, Lucerne and the beauty of the Austrian Alps.

Clifford remained in Bristol until the end of his life; he touched many people's lives by his charisma, his musical prowess, his utter dependability and his professionalism. Yet, he remained very self-effacing, quiet and calmly dignified, as he went about in the musical world he had made his own. People felt that such a man ought to be recognised for his worth and he was given some reward for his outstanding services, though many felt more should have been given for his exceptional contribution to music in general.

As the congregation assembled in the Great Hall of the University of Bristol on 10th July, 1975, Clifford's own music was being played on the organ, to the great enrichment of that splendid scene. He was conferred Master of Music, honoris causa, and deemed eminently worthy of the honour, in recognition of his outstanding 25 years' service at the Cathedral. This was a rare honour conferred by the St. Mark's Institute of Theology and reserved only for those who had given notable service in religious work. It was to give recognition to good works and achievements in the religious sphere, and entitled him to wear the St. Mark's hood.

Further, in 1989, the year of his retirement from Bristol Choral Society, he was given a similar award by the Bristol Polytechnic (now University of the West of England) and it pleased him greatly that the ceremony was held in Bristol Cathedral. At that auspicious ceremony, too, Clifford's own 'Rouen Processional' was played on the organ he had loved for so many years. In his speech of thanks, speaking confidently and warmly and fluently without any notes, he looked around and added "I love every stone in this place" which added a personal sentiment fitting for the occasion.

Thus ended Clifford Harker's working span; a time utterly absorbed in that which he loved - making music - yet not keeping it for himself or seeking self-esteem. The extraordinary influence he had of imparting a richness and beauty of music to others inspired everyone to become more aware of it for themselves and so to enjoy and appreciate it with an added dimension.

CHAPTER 2
PATHS UNTROD
'Today is thrilling'

From Newcastle to the Middle East

Attempting to envisage Clifford's thoughts as he considered his posting to the Canal Zone would, undoubtedly, echo the thoughts and apprehension of thousands of people who served in the armed forces during the war. Uprooted from the security of home, family, working routine and all things familiar and regular, the enforced military discipline, with little privacy, and a growing state of uncertainty, had to be endured by everyone concerned, of whatever rank or calling. The altogether different routine necessitated considerable adjustment for many. True, some found the life new and exciting - seeing far away places 'at His Majesty's expense', and the prospect of going all out to undo the enemy generated a battle-cry of "let's get it over with!" Others were very sensitive to what was going on but accepted the situation with calm determination and worked in the best way they knew for their own part in the effort needed to win the struggle for all freedom-loving people with crossed fingers for themselves. For - make no mistake - every adult and sane-thinking person knew that life would be very different for themselves, their country, and freedom of the peace-loving world, if the other side gained the upper hand. Many different factors led to victory for Britain and her allies and although this is not the place to recall the progress of the war, it is important to stress that each serving man and woman, and every thinking person, realised the undertaking.

Clifford Harker was as sensitive as the next person and, at the age of 27 or so, with a mature, down-to-earth determination, resolved to do his best for the sake of everyone's future. Nevertheless, like thousands of other service personnel, boarding a troopship for the Middle East gave him the sickening thought that he might never return to his native shores and all that had been dependable and secure.

It is easy, from present day viewpoint, knowing the outcome of the war and having some idea of Clifford's consequent destiny, to dismiss the situation lightly but at the time everything - just everything - was uncertain, even what the next day would bring. And so, aboard the troopship 'Samaria' (as with so many other sea-going vessels) morale needed to be kept high at all costs, and when Clifford realised he could do something to help this truly unsavoury situation, he got on with doing whatever he was good at.

Many young men, whilst enjoying a taste of adventure, were inwardly afraid and Clifford's work aboard ship went a long way to creating a more relaxed atmosphere in the midst of a nail-biting situation. His efforts in creating music (and it does not need a great deal of imagination to realise that even doing this could not have been at all easy - it was a troopship going to war, not a concert hall) were a positive response to the situation, resulting in a real uplifting of spirits for all on board. People would be taken mentally out of their tense situation as they sang and listened, and gradually there came a new spirit of enjoyment, of comradeship and sense of optimism as the long journey progressed.

Clifford's efforts to make music, however impossible it must have seemed in the beginning, had the happy result in some men discovering for the first time that they had a voice to sing with and produce a good sound - with a little help - or encouraged others to revive a long-lost skill and, as they came together to learn the pieces which Clifford had so competently written out by hand, even the manuscript paper. They sang lustily and cheerfully and forgot the imminent dangers for a time. Whether or not there was a piano on board is left to conjecture but, whatever the circumstances, Clifford excelled.

Thus, after successful and rewarding times aboard ship, and an exciting time music-making in Durban, the troopship 'Samaria' neared the Suez port. Great friendships had been forged at such times as these, and many would have parted with saddened hearts as the disembarkation started - the battalions, having at length found their sea-legs now prepared to recover their land-legs once more after six weeks at sea. Again, handshakes were firm and resolute, for none knew what the future held.

To many, the journey had been an exciting new part of their life - few had the chance to travel abroad in those days, and now the African Continent seemed an almost unreal world. On land everything looked so different - palm trees instead of the familiar oak, white sun-drenched buildings which dazzled the eye, and dusty roads, vivid blue skies and hot sun. It was a place to enjoy, certainly, but the enemy was not far away, and a very real threat. There was no four-star hotel awaiting the arrival of tourists but, for many, a bell-tent or, for the more fortunate, a rough wooden billet, with very little privacy. It was unusually hot and sticky with the constant presence of foreign flies and nasties; 'K.D.' was worn mostly, which made the knees even more vulnerable to bites! Cold at night, maybe, but how difficult to adjust to unfamiliar temperatures. And all the time there was the inescapable knowledge that the enemy was advancing fast along the northern coast of Africa, with the threat getting nearer by the hour. RAF units worked twenty-four hours a day, often with speedily trained mechanics, in a concerted effort to repair damaged aircraft - airframes and engines, in order to resume the task of keeping the enemy at bay. These units were constantly being identified by enemy reconnaissance aircraft, and became what was wryly termed 'the object of their attention'. Heavy bombing raids hit billets and stores, some men escaped only in what they were wearing; and lives were lost. Near Cairo, these tactics were continued until a bomb-proof place of safety was found in a deep cave in the nearby mountains where stone was quarried for cement making. Apparently, the caves were formed originally when the stone was quarried to build the Pyramids on the far side of the River Nile. It was in this kind of situation that Leading Aircraftman Harker expected to be working.

6. British Forces desert camp about 20 miles from Cairo.
7. Cairo Cathedral floodlit on V E Night.

In Cairo itself, people at first hardly knew there was a war on; the city was the normal bustle of people and activities. Resident there was a goodly number of Europeans who had worked there for some years and had formed a stable community. The main place for Christian worship was the Cathedral Church of All Saints, built in 1936 - a large building for a small community in the beginning but with its own mixed choir, and soon to become packed out during the war years, as it turned out. The resident clergy were the much-loved **Bishop Llewellyn Gwynne**, an elderly but saintly man and Bishop of Egypt and the Sudan, who spent his time between Cairo and Khartoum; his Archdeacon, the **Reverend Francis Johnston**, who later became Bishop; and the **Reverend Arthur Burrell**, Johnston's Assistant. Arthur and his wife, Pat, both joined Clifford's Choral Society. Incidentally, in 1974 the Cathedral was scheduled for demolition to make way for a wide new road through the centre of Cairo as an approach to a new bridge over the River Nile. With the full agreement of the Egyptian authorities, a new Cathedral was built, in a style more suitable for modern needs, in another part of the city.

King Farouk once went to see the Archdeacon at the Cathedral. He admired its beauty, remarking on the fine window grilles. On being told they were made of wood he offered to give gold metal grilles.

After the Battle of Britain the scene changed dramatically; there was a colossal build-up of forces from Britain and the countries of her Empire, bringing thousands of them to the area to be stationed, either in or nearby, or passing through the general headquarters in Cairo. There was much disarray with so many additional people in the area, but there was always good food to be had in the restaurants and, although the sirens sounded occasionally, no bombs dropped on the city. The enemy would not have minded bombing the British, but they did not want to upset the Egyptians, and thought better of destroying their capital although Cairo was full of 'intelligence'.

Cairo was a beautiful, modern, Egyptian city with many noteworthy attractions: it had a well-known opera house for which Verdi had written his opera 'Aida' at the grand opening of the Suez Canal; it had zoological gardens with a large lake and island restaurant, and many important buildings.

September, 1941. Clifford's arrival was a godsend to Cairo. Within a few weeks he had re-formed his Services Choral Society (men's), about fifty strong and gave a first performance in the Cathedral Hall with Choir Accompanist **Roger Wilson** (described as always humble, versatile and untiring). The two men had met and forged a partnership on the troopship on the way to the Middle East. He was organ soloist at some of Clifford's concerts later on, and he and Clifford sometimes played piano duets at recitals.

An account of the first concert, written by Archdeacon Johnston, in the Egypt and Sudan Diocesan Review, October, 1941 reads: 'Aircraftman Clifford Harker, F.R.C.O., A.R.C.M., sometime sub-organist at Newcastle

Top left: 8. Bishop Llewellyn Gwynne.
Top right: 9. Archdeacon Francis Johnston.
Bottom left: 10. Rev. Arthur Burrell.
Bottom Right: 11. Relaxing on the Cathedral steps
(a change from organ pipes).

Cathedral and leader of various Bach choirs in the north of England, is now stationed in Cairo and has identified himself with the work of the Cathedral. On Sunday, 28th September he gave an organ recital before the Evening Service, the programme including some of his own compositions. On the invitation of our own organist he played for the Service the same evening. Clifford Harker is now forming a Services Choral Society, the practices taking place in the Cathedral Hall on Monday evenings at 9 p.m., and Friday afternoons at 2.30 p.m. The first concert is to be held in the Hall on Sunday evening, October 19th.' The choir gave its first performance to an audience of 500, and the programme consisted of carefully rehearsed arrangements of folk songs such as 'Lass of Richmond Hill', 'Solomon Levi', and 'Down in Demerara' (which, no doubt, Clifford had so laboriously written and harmonised for his ship's choir). According to the Egyptian Gazette of December 1st, 1941, the songs 'proved so popular with the appreciative audience that, with friendly charm, Mr. Harker explained that, as the choir had rehearsed them so strenuously and they were so short - they would sing them again - and they did, to the entire approval of all listeners'. In the same report, the reporter also remarked "I watched the audience file out at the end. In the crowd I saw captains and privates, sergeants and lieutenants, padres and aircraftmen, and so on. They had been drawn together to enjoy something they would all share equally - good music, comfort and quiet, tasteful surroundings".

As concerts and recitals continued at the rate of one each month, Clifford arranged more folk songs, student songs and sea shanties, and included some of his own compositions - all inspired by his choir.

Music for All

'Music for All' was a music and leisure centre, founded by **Lady Dorothea Russell**, with a group of ladies resident in Cairo. Her husband was Chief of the Egyptian Police. The Centre was in 3 Sharia Maarouf and consisted of a good sized concert hall converted from an old cinema, a number of rooms of various sizes which were comfortably furnished and used as reading rooms, quiet rooms, and rooms where people could chat or play cards, and so on. Also in the complex was a good quality restaurant, run by the high class Egyptian catering firm 'Groppi', and sheltered, peaceful gardens for relaxing. The centre had become a welcome haven for service people in Cairo; most were passing through with their units, or visiting from outlying nearby camps - such as the ones mentioned above, which were suffering enemy frequent bombardment. Lady Russell had done much for people's comfort and rehabilitation and temporary relief from the tumult of war in the surrounding area. She was regarded as quite a formidable lady, but she worked hard and showed a true, caring, spirit. The Centre was open to all Allied Forces, whatever their rank. It was a meeting place where everyone was equal and rank was disregarded.

12. Chareh Maarouf, 'Music for All' sign.
13. 'A La Groppi' restaurant in 'Music for All' Centre.
14. The North Garden at 'Music for All'

When the Centre was opened, five months earlier, Lady Dorothea appointed **Gerhard Willner**, a pianist and musician, but as enemy troops reached El Alamein and became a threat to Cairo itself, his nationality made it diplomatic for him to leave for South Africa. Thus, someone was vitally needed for the organisation of the music at the Centre. Clifford's work aboard ship and his successful concerts in Durban and Cairo had been brought to the notice of the authorities in the Canal Zone, and so he was approached as being eminently suitable to take on the Centre. **Group Captain (Teddy) Evans**, O.B.E., arranged for Clifford's secondment and, before long, he became full time Director of Music.

In January, 1942, Clifford (now Corporal) became organist and choirmaster at the Cathedral, and about the same time he formed a Ladies Choral Society, consisting of members of the three services as well as resident civilians. This enabled him to become more ambitious with choral works and some of the first concerts given by the combined societies were held in the Cathedral. The programmes included chorales from Bach's St. Matthew Passion. Twice-weekly rehearsals were held in the Cathedral Hall throughout the whole period.

May, 1942 saw the combined choirs enjoying the lighter side of music when they sang choruses from Gilbert and Sullivan operas, and the 'Soldiers' Chorus' from Gounod's Faust, whilst competent soloists added even more variety.

At the Cathedral, Clifford was becoming a regular organist and recitalist and in **September, 1942**, he played the instrument at a Memorial Service for the **Duke of Kent**, who had been killed in action; his rendering of Chopin's 'Funeral March' at the end of the service was regarded as a fitting close to a moving and dignified tribute to the Duke's memory. One soldier was heard to say on leaving the Cathedral that it had done more to strengthen his hope of the hereafter than all the creeds he had learnt. Such was Clifford's influence in his style of playing. That same evening, the combined societies gave a choral recital on the steps of the Cathedral, which included 'This Joyful Eastertide', 'Deck Thyself', Bach's Passion Chorale 'O Sacred Head' and 'Bread of the World'. This last piece was used by Clifford at many services and performances and may well have been his own setting, published later.

The newspaper reporter of 'The Sphinx' commented "the more that can be seen and heard of a choir of this standard, the better. A large proportion of the audience were servicemen, thus confounding those who seem to imagine that all people in uniform are interested only in the more banal products of Hollywood".

Training and performing with his choirs was only a part of Clifford's work and even this was not always easy. He fully realised that they were at war; the chorus members had their duties which could be changed at any time, and members could even be posted elsewhere at a moment's notice; the orchestra could not rehearse as often as they wished, and there was always the provision of music to be organised somehow as finding copies for ninety to one hundred people was no mean task - much midnight oil was burned by willing helpers turning the old duplicator. In addition he was responsible for daily recitals at the Music for All Centre. He arranged chamber and piano recitals, often performing himself, and gramophone recitals when a live performance was not possible. This necessitated much time in administration and quiet arranging of concerts, and music parts. Somehow, in between, he managed to continue his studies for an external degree, sending completed work to tutors whenever possible. A remarkable timetable for Corporal Harker!

Thus, Clifford became immersed day and night, almost, in his one passion! Not content with concerts of selected items, however, he set his sights on one-work performances with his choir.

September, 1942, Handel's 'Messiah' was the first of the more ambitious works to be tackled, always popular with audiences and a favourite with himself. Publicity brought much excitement to the venture, even photographs of rehearsals taking place were published in the press. 'Messiah' was performed in the Cathedral on two occasions in September, and once at the Centre. 1942 was a great year, and these were great occasions for many people connected with Clifford's choirs.

This was the first ever performance in Egypt with full orchestra which included woodwind and brass from the Cairo Area Military Band, and three solo singers. There had been a performance on a smaller scale, conducted by Sir Arthur Sullivan, about seventy years previously. The Cathedral was never known to be so full, with heads peering through the narrow gaps high up in the dome. As well as a crammed Cathedral, people were sitting outside on the grass in the precincts near the large open-grilled windows, on two very stiflingly hot nights. Amongst the dignitaries in the audience were **Prince George of Greece** (later King), and **Air Chief Marshall Tedder**, who ordered that air raid sirens be sounded only in dire emergency. Fortunately, everything went off without a visit from the enemy, though the sirens sounded frequently in the capital at other times, without any actual raid.

The press was abundant in its praise; the choir was described as 'magnificent' and 'seldom has the always-thrilling 'for unto us' sounded more thrilling, or the Hallelujah Chorus given with more fire - the congregation seemed to be almost breathless after it'. Clifford 'conducted with mastery and enthusiasm' and 'Cairo owes much to Clifford Harker'.

Such deserved success brought Clifford much acclaim from his own choir; so thrilled and grateful were they that his genius had carried them to heights of sonority rarely felt, that their excitement knew no bounds. Afterwards Clifford was chaired and carried round shoulder high in procession, whilst everybody sang "For he's a jolly good fellow". Later, he was presented with an inscribed leather-bound album containing the signatures of all those taking part, which included all the singers, and players,

15. 'Music for All' concert.

16. Front of 'Messiah' programme.
Notice the musical quotation – a very shrewd heading to all the MFA programmes. Were these bars of Beethoven's fifth symphony the famous V-for-Victory beat of all the Allies in wartime, or the rhythm of 'Music for All'? Probably both.

some of whom had played in such orchestras as the London Philharmonia Orchestra, the London Symphony Orchestra, the Hallé Orchestra and the Auckland Philharmonic Orchestra, before becoming servicemen. There were photographs of the Choir, the Cathedral, Cathedral clergy, and it was a gift much treasured for the remainder of his life.

Even the British News got to hear of it, and extracts of the performance came through on the wireless, with descriptions of the scene by the well-known broadcaster, Godfrey Talbot, after the 1 o'clock News. Clifford's father, Arthur, was interviewed at his home in Cavendish Place, Newcastle, and he commented that "It was a great thrill and surprise, for we knew about it only a few hours before. Clifford has been in the RAF for about eighteen months". Arthur Harker managed to get a local news cutting through to his son, on which he wrote 'H. Hudson's note. Please thank him. Everybody thrilled by broadcast. Cheerio. Have written. All well. Dad'.

It seems that everyone who took part in this and all performances that Clifford organised, received permanent and priceless memories of a time of great inspiration and pleasure.

Clifford himself was always to retain this as a much cherished memory and recalled it many times during his life for, never in his wildest dreams, could he have imagined that he would find himself conducting 'Messiah' in Egypt. One lasting picture he kept in his mind's eye was of a group of wounded and blinded Australian servicemen sitting in the audience as he turned to bring the people in the audience to their feet for the Hallelujah Chorus. He never conducted the Hallelujah Chorus afterwards without this memory returning. The performance touched many people in a variety of ways, and the people of Cairo openly felt that the Forces Welfare Committee had shown exceptional enlightenment in employing Clifford Harker in a musical, rather than a strictly military role. Maybe a more efficient wireless operator was sent to replace Clifford, but Clifford certainly became irreplaceable in his role for the remainder of his time in Cairo! ...... and now he had become Flight Sergeant Harker.

1943 The choir's response to Clifford's leadership was assured and went from strength to strength, with a concert version of Edward German's 'Merrie England' in addition to other concerts; Christmas Music at the Cathedral and Brahms' 'Requiem' in April, 1944.

1944 June brought a recital of church music in the Cathedral, with chorus items, organ solos given by Roger Wilson, and concluded with a six-fold Amen written by Clifford and sung by the male chorus. In November, six concert performances of John Gay's 'The Beggar's Opera' were given at Music for All, with string trio and Clifford directing from the piano. During November, 1944, two performances of Haydn's 'The Creation' were given at the Cathedral to crowded congregations.

These performances were, indeed, great achievements for, it should be remembered that with the choir consisting of frequently changing personnel, new choir members needed to be trained and nurtured into the

17. Men's Choral Society rehearsal.
18. Choral rehearsal in Cairo Cathedral

body, and time was needed for the music to be learned - with much forbearance on the part of the conductor. Nevertheless, because of changes in personnel, Clifford touched the lives of even more people who would always remain thankful for the experience.

E.N.S.A. To some extent, ENSA was involved in the Music for All project, and this brought professional performers with their capable expertise; many of these people were amazed at the work which Clifford was doing in that part of the world, and under such difficult circumstances. The Middle East Symphony Orchestra visited under the auspices of ENSA, and Clifford was invited to conduct an all-Bach concert, which included the B minor suite, the double violin concerto, the violin concerto in E and the fifth Brandenburg concerto for flute, violin, piano and strings: a particular achievement for Clifford and one which brought further invitations.

December, 1944, brought Nativity Tableaux with carols and a fine Carol Service with excerpts from 'Messiah', given by the Choral Societies and the Middle East Light Symphony Orchestra. This time there were solos by a young Flying Officer, **Arthur Reckless**, recently arrived in the area, with a superb baritone voice. Arthur had performed successfully at Queen's Hall and the National Gallery concerts in London. Thirty years later Arthur Reckless recalled his first meeting with Clifford: he had been invited to perform for Music for All, and Clifford's approach was friendly, but cautious - as a musical director would be to a performer with 'pure white knees'. He asked Reckless "What can you do?". Reckless replied that he thought he could sing - and that he had recently performed at the Henry Wood Promenade concerts. This proved the requisite 'passport', and many successful performances followed whilst Reckless was in the Canal Zone. The two men became firm friends and after the war Arthur Reckless became a sought-after baritone and sang for Clifford at Rugby in some of the great choral works. It was, in fact, he who succeeded Clifford at Music for All when Clifford returned home for demobilisation.

1945 Clifford's name became familiar in Middle Eastern musical circles and he was invited to accompany recitalists when they visited Music for All, and even further afield in Alexandria. **Dr. Thomas Armstrong**, who had toured the Middle East forces, studying cultural and educational activities after the end of hostilities, commented in his report to 'The Times' of his admiration for those who had made strenuous efforts to provide centres of live music. He mentioned Clifford Harker (who had by then been promoted to the rank of Warrant Officer) whom he had seen conducting the **Palestine Symphony Orchestra** (which Clifford was to do on a number of occasions whilst still in the Middle East).

The **Palestine Orchestra** was a body of professional musicians and Clifford conducted them on three occasions at Music for All. He had much success with the players and subsequently travelled to **Jerusalem**, **Haifa** and **Tel Aviv** to conduct them in these three Middle East cities. At each concert the same programme was given: Handel: Water Music, Mozart: Symphony in

19. Press photograph in the Report of 'Messiah' performance.

20. Arthur Reckless

E flat major, Brahms: Haydn Variations and Weber: Overture 'Oberon'. The conductor wore RAF uniform. In **February, 1945**, the Palestine Post reported the concert: '.......a young musician with distinct gifts ......a tasteful selection, tastefully executed. With a tone or two more colour, Mr. Harker, who is at the outset of his career, should make his way as a conductor'.

Following the tour, a letter of appreciation arrived from the Palestine Orchestra Administrator:

>Tel Aviv
>27th August, 1945
>
>Now that the war is over I think that it will not be very long before your wish to go back to England will be fulfilled. May I take this opportunity to thank you very much for all you have done for the Palestine Orchestra, not only in your capacity as Music Director of "Music for All" but also as conductor.
>
>All of us, the Orchestra, & the undersigned, appreciate highly your musicianship and your gift for leading and controlling an orchestra and thus being able to obtain the finest artistic results. We are only sorry that your duties did not allow you more opportunities to conduct our ensemble in Egypt .....press, public and ourselves all obtained the impression that a successful future as a conductor lies before you .... we hope we shall have the pleasure of having you in Palestine once again and conducting the orchestra.
>
>Very sincerely yours,
>(sgd) S.B.Lewertoff, Administrator

Continuing with his work at Music for All, Clifford produced 'Polly' by John Gay in a costumed concert version, Stanford's 'Songs of the Fleet', with Clifford's own light chorus songs 'Flowers of the Valley', 'Diaphenia' and 'The Owl and the Pussy Cat'. There was a concert version of Gilbert and Sullivan's 'Iolanthe' and concert performances of John Gay's 'The Beggar's Opera' at Music for All, and in Alexandria (for ENSA).

In **May, 1945**, Clifford was involved in an unusual occasion; there was a competition for Forces composers, organised by ENSA Good Music Section. Clifford was asked to conduct some of the entries with the Middle East Symphony Orchestra in a concert of the prize-winning works, which was broadcast for the benefit of music lovers outside Cairo.

Now the sojourn in Egypt was coming to an end. Clifford was due to return to England for demobilisation and so two farewell concerts in his honour were planned at Music for All. Four years had passed since he had formed the choirs and now they were being disbanded - a sad time in many ways for all concerned. Hundreds of singers had passed through his hands

"Songs of the Fleet" performance.
September 1943. Cairo.

21. Sketch of you know who! (unsigned).

deriving great pleasure from it - something he was to cause to happen for many years to come.

1945. September 22 and 23, Farewell Concerts

Needless to say, everyone taking part in the **Farewell Concerts** gave their all, not least Clifford, because it marked the disbanding of the Ladies' and Services' Choral Societies after exactly four years of wonderfully uplifting music making. Many were soon to return home for demobilisation, and to attempt to carry on without good numbers and with less satisfying results, it was better to cease whilst conditions were at their zenith. The final concert, whilst bitter-sweet for most, delighted everyone present.

On Sunday evening, 30th September, 1945, the Choral Society augmented the Cathedral Choir and sang Evening Prayers with particular effusion. The service included Bach's harmonisation of the hymn tune 'Innsbruch' to the words 'The duteous day now closeth'; Psalm 150 to Stanford; the anthem 'Jesu, joy of man's desiring' (Bach) and ended with Clifford's setting of the words 'O Lord, support us all the day long of this troublous life, until the shades lengthen, and the evening comes, and the busy world is hushed, the fever of life is over, and our work is done. Then, Lord, in thy mercy, grant us safe lodging, a holy rest, and peace at the last.' Clifford's six-fold Amen followed the Blessing.

So ended a chapter of Clifford's life, one which would for ever remain a time of success and rich blessing; the high-note of his life in many respects - for through his ineffective wireless operating he had more than successfully communicated something which he was expert at achieving - the giving of musical pleasure to others. And, in the rigours of war, not only giving pleasure but a stirring of the spirit which enabled thousands of others to continue the battle with spirits high and courage strong.

Much tribute was paid to Clifford for his work and he was given a Memento put together by the Ladies' and Men's Choral Societies after the performance of 'Messiah' in appreciation of his leadership: '....despite many handicaps, carried on unwaveringly through the recent crisis, and brought to a successful conclusion the production of 'Messiah' .... we have in our temporary exile, ourselves found solace and inspiration as well as the joy of passing on to others his scholarly renderings of the true essence and spirit of all that is best in British music ....to achieve a thing of beauty which to all of us will be a treasured memory and, to many others, a joy for ever ......
HEIL HARKER !

'Esteban' of the 'Sphinx', in his account of the Farewell concert said 'Providence has decreed that good should come out of evil and we should be thankful for it. There should therefore be no surprise that the war sent us a Clifford Harker. .....the reverse is also true, for when the war is over the good things have to disappear with the evil and the time has now come for us to say "goodbye".' He referred to the performances of 'Messiah' which 'had not only coincided with the bicentenary of the oratorio, but was also a mighty gesture in defiance of the Hun, who was then actually at our gates. I have often wondered whether Rommel heard about it, for the spirit it displayed could not have been much to his liking. Not only does he leave us with this enhanced reputation but also with the grateful thanks of thousands into whose lives - possibly for the first time - has come the solace of music.'

Letters of appreciation accompanied Clifford as he departed Cairo in November, 1945. Archdeacon Francis Johnston's made reference to the difference he had made to the normal services, adding new life and a richness of worship; and he spoke of 'inspired leadership'. The Bishop of Egypt, Llewellyn Gwynne, sent him home with a glowing testimonial to the effect that the Services, which had drawn thousands of men and women of the forces to worship had been due to his artistic skill and devotion. He had formed a choral society, of which members of the Cathedral Choir had been a part, and had enabled crowds to enjoy the great musical works, making a great name for himself as a conductor all through the Middle East.

Some time later Clifford was to receive the small gift of an illustrated book entitled 'Cathedral on the Nile' written by his colleague in Cairo, Arthur Burrell. It described the Cathedral in Cairo, the work of its clergy and members there, and it made glowing reference to Clifford as organist during the war, together with his photograph.

The journey home was devoid of the dangers of the outward trip (and there could even have been music on the voyage - who knows?). It gave Clifford the pleasure of resting on his laurels, and recalling the relationships and friendships formed and debts to all with whom he had worked in Cairo. He was to recall the most senior ranking RAF officer, Air Chief Marshall Tedder, who had cheerfully served Christmas Dinner to the men in a long tent erected out in the street; and later, the same man, distraught with grief, as the funeral service of his wife was held in the Cathedral, after she had been killed in an air crash, Clifford playing for the service. The gratitude would include not only those he knew, but others who had provided the grounding he had received in preparation for his musical career, and those who had given him the chance to prove himself before joining up. Most of all, thoughts of home and his dear father, who was no longer there to welcome him and share his successes and memories, nor his beloved brother. So the feelings were very mixed as at length he sighted the shores of England again.

After four years in the hot climate of Egypt, with endless sun, endless music, and the stimulation of becoming a successful and popular figure, the sight of England, now drab in the throes of winter, was somewhat comfortless to Clifford and, like so many others, readjustment took time and conscious effort.

It will not be out of place to insert here more detail of the extent of Clifford's work in the Middle East.

As already recorded he was occupied with Music for All in many ways, and with the Cathedral, but in addition to his activities with his choirs he was greatly engrossed in writing choral arrangements, studying orchestral scores for concerts and preparing for a number of recitals with visiting artistes; continuing, also, with his own studies, so it is no wonder there was never a dull moment.

It is interesting to discover that the note 'arr.C.H.' appeared so many years before Bristol.

Music for Cairo Choirs
Part song arrangements:
1941   Lass of Richmond Hill
        Solomon Levi
        Down in Demerara
1942   Ye banks and braes
        All through the night
        A hundred pipers
        The Mermaid
        Annie Laurie (Scottish)
1943   Loch Lomond
        Skye Boat Song
        Shenandoah
        Riding down from Bangor
        True Love
        The meeting of the waters
1944   Vive l'Amour
        Dashing away with the smoothing iron
        My Lord, what a morning
        Going Home
        The Water of Tyne
        My love's an arbutus
1945   Blow away the morning dew
        Bobby Shaftoe

1945 Original work
        Four Light Songs (SATB, orchestrated)
                Flowers in the valley
                Diaphenia
                The owl and the pussy cat
                The Jumblies

Sacred
1942   Christus natus hodie (mixed voices) words Arthur Burrell,
                                Music by C.H.
        The Russian Kontakion for the departed
        A Babe is born in Bethlehem (orchestrated)
        Silent Night (for male voices, and SATB)
        Shepherds in the fields abiding (male voices, and SATB)
1943   King Jesus hath a garden (male voices, and SATB)

1944
O Lord, support us all the day long
Whence is that goodly fragrance
The noble stem of Jesse
I saw three ships
Christ was born on Christmas Day
What Child is this?
Whom of old the shepherds praised
The Holly and the Ivy
In dulci jubilo
We Three Kings
Unto us is born a Son
Silent Night (arr. for soprano solo)
When Christ was born of Mary free
Sixfold AMEN

....

C.H. The Conductor

Clifford was able to expand his experience as an orchestral conductor during his years in Cairo. The following is a résumé of the works he performed with an *ad hoc* chamber group, The Middle East Light Symphony Orchestra, and the Palestine Orchestra, in Music for All and elsewhere (as indicated):

1942 Sept/Oct	Handel: Messiah (3 performances)	
1943 Feb.	German: Merrie England (4 performances)	
1944 Jan.	Palestine Symphony Orchestra and piano soloists from ENSA:	
	Bach: Suite No. 3 in D	
	Bach: Concerto in C for 2 pianos and string orchestra	
	Beethoven: Symphony No. 5 in C minor	
1944 April	Brahms: Requiem (3 performances)	
1944 Nov.	Gay: The Beggar's Opera (6 performances with piano and string trio)	
1944 Nov.	Haydn: The Creation (2 performances) with Middle East SO	
1944 Nov.	Handel: Water Music Suite	
	Haydn: Symphony No. 104 (London)	
	Schubert: Entracte & Ballet Music from 'Rosamunde'	
	Mendelssohn: Overture 'The Hebrides'	
1944 Dec.	Bach/Mozart Festival (ENSA), with Middle East SO.	
	Bach: B minor Suite, Double Violin Concerto, Violin Concerto in E,	
	Brandenberg Concerto No. 5	

1945 Jan.   at Music for All.
Palestine Symphony Orchestra, with
George Themeli, piano
Mozart: Symphony No. 39 in E flat
Beethoven: Concerto No. 5 in E flat (The Emperor) for piano and orchestra

1945 Feb.   with Palestine Orchestra in Jerusalem (Edison Hall), Tel Aviv (Ohel Hall) and Haifa (Armon Theatre)
Handel: Water Music Suite
Mozart: Symphony in E flat major (K.543)
Brahms: Variations on a theme by Haydn (St. Anthony Chorale)
Weber: Overture 'Oberon'

1945 April at Music for All with Palestine Symphony Orchestra and Arthur Reckless
Mozart: Serenade in G major (Eine Kleine Nachtmusik)
Mozart: Symphony No. 40 in G minor
Handel: Recitative and Aria from 'Messiah' 'For behold, darkness' and 'The People that walked'
Mendelssohn: Overture 'The Hebrides'

1945 April   Gay: 'Polly' at Music for All

1945 May   Middle East Forces Composers' Competition
CH conducted Finalists' Concert with Middle East Symphony Orchestra (59 players) at the Garrison Theatre, Cairo. The orchestra included locally based players, members of Cairo Military Band, personnel of RAF and members of the Egyptian Royal Bodyguard Band
  Anthony Lewis: Two City Dances
  Anthony Smith-Masters: A Berkshire Idyll
  Stephen O'Reilley: Three Miniatures
  Robert Jones: Idyll for Soprano and Strings 'The Late Lark'
  Michael Vickers: Ballet Suite 'The Chessmen'
  Loraine White: Three Impressions for Piano and Orchestra
  Harry Dexter: 'Nocturne' (2nd Movement from Symphony in G)
  John Harrison: Avon Suite

1945 July at Music for All, with Middle East Light Symphony Orchestra, Choral Societies and Arthur Reckless (Baritone)

Weber: Overture 'Euryanthe'
Choir Items (unacc.)
Borodin: Prince Igor's aria (solo) (orch. CH)
Eric Coates: Two Symphonic Rhapsodies (Orchestra)
 I pitch my lonely caravan
 Bird Songs at Eventide
Mozart: Overture 'The Marriage of Figaro'
Choir items (unacc.)
Two items for Baritone soloist and piano:
 Mallinson: Eleanore
 Hely-Hutchinson: Song of Soldiers
Choir items with orchestra

1945 Sept. 22 & 23 Two Farewell Concerts by the Combined Ladies' and Services' Choral Societies, with the Middle East Light Symphony Orchestra and Arthur Reckless

The National Anthem
Choir and Orchestra: O Faith of England (words T.A.Lacey)
 Genevan Psalm Tune, 1525
Four British Folk Songs (unacc.) arr. CH
 My love's an Arbutus (Irish)
 Blow away the morning dew (Somersetshire)
 Annie Laurie (Scottish)
 Bobby Shaftoe (Northumbrian)
Orchestra: Delibes: Ballet Music 'Sylvia'
Solo, chorus and orchestra: Selection from Stanford's
 Songs of the Fleet
Choir: Mozart: Ave Verum (unacc.)
Choir: Bach: Jesu, joy of man's desiring (with
 orchestra)
Solo: Borodin: Prince Igor's Aria (with orch. arr. CH)
Choir and Orchestra: Harker: Four Light Songs

  . . . .

C.H. - Pianist and Accompanist

1942 Feb. At the Anglo-Egyptian Union, Cairo:
 Original compositions for piano:
  1) Rosalie
  2) Lullaby

1943 Dec. **Cello Recital** with **Regine Schein** for the Egyptian Music Society in the Oriental Hall (American University)
 H.E. Eccles: Sonate en sol mineur
 J.S. Bach: Adagio
 Tartini-Stutschewsky: Sonate en la majeur
 E. Bloch: Méditation Hébraique
 Albeniz-Stutschewsky: Malaguena
 F. Chopin: Nocturne

     G. Cassado: Requiebros (Danse Espagnole)

1944 May **Recital** with **Hanna Starer (soprano)** at Music
        for All
    Piano: Schubert: Impromptu Op. 142 No. 2.
        Mozart: Sonata No. 6 in F
        Brahms: from Six Piano Pieces, Op. 118
         No. 5 Romanze
         No. 3 Ballade
      Schumann: from Phantasie-stucke Op. 12
        Warum
        Aufschwung
   With Soprano: Schubert: Four songs:
        Geheimes Du bist die ruh
        Ganymed Musensohn
       Rossini: Rosina's aria from 'The
         Barber of Seville'
       Verdi: Violetta's aria from
         'La Traviata'
1944 Oct. **Recital** with **Irene Drakides, violin,** at
  Montgomery House, Alexandria (similar to Music for All)
    piano: Brahms: Ballade Op. 118 No. 3
        Intermezzo Op. 117 No. 1
        Rhapsody Op. 119 No. 4
   with violin: Vivaldi: Concerto in A minor (1680)
       Corelli: Sonata in E minor (1655)
       Mozart: Sonata in E minor (1778)
       Mozart: Sonata in A major (1778)
1944 Oct. **Recital** with **Taki Kyriakides, baritone** (with own
      accompanist) at Music for All
  Bach: Choral Preludes 'Sleepers wake, a voice is calling'
  Mozart: Sonata in F
  Chopin: Two Preludes: 1) C minor 2) D flat major
  Brahms: Two pieces: 1) Intermezzo in E flat, Op. 117 No. 1
        2) Rhapsody in E flat, Op. 119 No. 4
    . . . .

Rugby
  Life was now to take a different turn and Clifford, as with countless others leaving the Forces, now had to look for, and find, suitable employment. Doubtless, he kept his organ fingers and feet busy somewhere whilst waiting for a suitable post. How glad he was that throughout all the busy-ness of his RAF period, he had managed to continue with his own studies for a Bachelor of Music degree. Throughout the war years, somehow the completed and marked papers passed between him and his helpful tutor, **Dr. Ben Burrows**. Clifford could not have studied with a better man for Dr. Burrows was careful

to discourage composition that was merely striving for effect and would not stand the test of time. Based in nearby Leicester, Dr. Burrows was a teacher and composer of renown, who travelled extensively in his work. He was organist at Victoria Road Baptist Church, Leicester, for many years and was himself no mean composer. His own works included Chorale Preludes for organ, anthems, compositions for piano, art songs (set to classic poets) and psalm settings.

It was a proud moment when Clifford received his **Bachelor of Music degree from Durham University** - a further triumph in his burgeoning career and a mark of encouragement, confirming his outstanding musical ability.

It did not take long to secure what Clifford felt would be a good move. It was to the **Parish Church of St. Andrew's, Rugby** (where the incumbent was the **Rev. Canon H.W. Baines**) that he made his way soon after demobilisation, and he arrived in Rugby, a small town in the Midlands county of Warwickshire, keenly anticipating the new phase of post-war life.

In addition to the organ and choir of the church, Clifford gave piano lessons on several days each week at **Trinity College, London**, and taught classes at the reputable **Lawrence Sheriff Grammar School in Rugby**. His home was a room at the Royal George Hotel in Rugby and very soon he began to exert his influence on those around him. Unhappily, he found that he did not enjoy class teaching, although he did a fine job and enthused many of the pupils to an understanding and love of music, and he was remembered with affection by those he taught, who would watch his tall figure scurrying about the school with teaching gown flying behind him in the wind (in stark contrast to the accepted manner of the rest of the staff who circumvented the school with a more dignified gait). Neither did he find fulfilment in teaching piano and it was **Dame Myra Hess**, who was also on the staff at Trinity, who turned a sympathetic ear to this young man and advised that he should not continue in a career which, for him, was not gratifying. Nevertheless, his time at Rugby was well spent and he did find pleasure in his work there. He led the church choir in his customary way, and his musical contribution to the services was always to create a worshipful atmosphere. He also gave regular monthly organ recitals at the church, some of which were broadcast on the Midland Home Service.

Clifford was remembered with affection by those whom he knew during the Rugby period, his compositions were popular - the 'Laudate Dominum' and 'Holy Father, cheer our way' in particular, and this piece, together with his 'Communion Service in G' were still being used regularly (becoming quite dog-eared with time and use) up to the time of writing this book.

Not content without large forces of choral singers, Clifford set about forming a choral society, which was named **The Rugby Singers**. This was a highly successful enterprise, and soon he had the joy of lifting his baton again to a substantial body of people who were keen to sing. Works performed included those of the popular choral repertoire:- Handel's Messiah, Mendelssohn's Elijah, Haydn's 'The Creation'. His good friend Arthur Reckless was invited to sing in a performance of Dvorak's 'Stabat Mater' on one occasion. This time it was not to effect a spirit of encouragement in time of war, but it did help to act as a tonic to refresh and revive the spirits of people still floundering in the frustrating effects of a cruel war. Music-making became an antidote, just as it had proved a soothing *entr'acte* for so many thousands in the Middle East.

In the four years that Clifford lived in Rugby he served the church admirably, found gratification in his choral society and made the best of life as he found it there. There was some free time, naturally, and his good friend, John Bennett, who had returned to his home in Northampton would cycle over to Rugby and together they would take long cycle rides exploring the countryside around. Despite lacking in cycling expertise, Clifford regarded these outings as great fun, and recreation like this served to give him some necessary relaxation of mind, together with good physical exercise. The young men also had at least one holiday at Lake Lucerne in Switzerland.

It is likely that through his friendship with **Alwyn Surplice** Clifford got to know about the vacancy at **Bristol Cathedral**. Alwyn held the post for several years after his war service and was moving to St. George's, Windsor; undoubtedly, he would have told Clifford about the move. However it happened, Clifford felt the call to the life, and so the Cathedral authorities were approached, resulting in his appointment.

22. Cairo Cathedral Choir, 1942. (Clifford in uniform)

CHAPTER 3
BRISTOL
'Intrepid you hear us cry'

1949 - and it was "Go west, lad" for Clifford! He moved south-west to the seafaring city of Bristol, with its busy port and wealth of history.

Undoubtedly, he had visited the city before on occasions but now that it was to become his home it deserved closer and more detailed exploration.

Described as 'the most beautiful city in England' by **John Betjeman**, it was not difficult to understand why the writer came to make such a sweeping statement. Bristol had been a busy water side settlement since early times and had, over hundreds of years, become a flourishing port, vessels negotiating the meandering tidal River Avon until they reached the Severn Estuary. There was thriving overseas trade from the 14th century, particularly the wine trade and spice trade between Bristol and the West Indies. Merchants became rich, built themselves fine houses and poured money into handsome buildings; even in modern times the heart of the city retained its mediaeval look until the 1920s. The atmosphere of those far-off days still survived in the King Street area, notably the inn Llandoger Trow and the 18th century Theatre Royal. The later Regency crescents in Clifton, with terraces overlooking the Avon Gorge, not to mention the Victorian and Edwardian buildings, the lovely Downs and open spaces, the famous zoo, a number of fine-looking schools and colleges, the Perpendicular style University tower, and the beginnings of a huge monumental classic Council House taking shape (finished after the war) - all told a story of an opulent past and of the development of a prosperous and important city.

The churches, too, seemed numberless, with dozens of spires and ecclesiastical facades to be seen, (some having been built on the old City Wall) both ornamental and traditional, with breathtaking architecture, together with the plainer non-Conformist styles of churches which had developed out of the more evangelical schools of thought in the 18th century.

All this Clifford drank in with pleasure and satisfaction - here was, indeed, a great heritage and, (near to his own heart) was the knowledge that Bristol could boast the first performance of Handel's 'Messiah' to take place in an English church in 1758 - with John Wesley in the congregation. But it was the Cathedral, steeped in history itself, which drew him most of all.

He knew Bristol before moving to that great city, but the setting which confronted him was not quite so idyllic. The City had suffered greatly in the war and it was many years before the damaged buildings could be restored to anything like their former beauty. The illustrious Cathedral, despite having escaped a direct hit, showed its own wounds: a 1,000 pound bomb had exploded on College Green, shattering the windows along the north side, and in the few lean years since the bombing, the Cathedral still showed scars of war, only gradually to be fully restored as funds became available.

The original priceless stained glass windows had been removed for safety, being replaced by plain glass, and it was these windows which were blown out in the bomb blast. One new window on that side of the Cathedral pays tribute to faithful Firewatchers who, during air raids, went on to the Cathedral roof and, with exceptional courage, caught hold of incendiary bombs landing there and hurled them down to the ground. Through these uncommonly brave people the Cathedral remained far less damaged than it might have been. One good thing that came out of all this was that when the original windows were put back they were arranged with more plain glass, and so let in much light and sunshine, making the interior light and bright and far more attractive than formerly, when the stained glass, beautiful though it was, had made the place much darker and more sombre.

To Clifford Harker, gazing on the magnificent building, it took on an immediate affinity: here was the place he could spend his days in working out his calling.

As he viewed the handsome twin towers and imposing West Front, the Cathedral looked as it had done since 1897, but its story stretched far back into the annals of time; back through sixteenth century restoration when, in 1542, it was designated Cathedral following the Dissolution of the Monasteries in 1539. He surveyed the buildings of the Cathedral School, now much extended, where, in 1542, some of its pupils were the original choristers. The Cathedral's history retreated further back still, to its founding by Robert Fitzhardinge as St.Augustine's Abbey and a centre of worship and learning, about 1140. He could even trace these beginnings as he particularly studied the Abbey Gatehouse and Chapter House (one of the finest Norman rooms in England) - visible evidence of Norman origins - and he decided there and then to find out more about the saintly Augustine, a Roman monk who converted the English to Christianity, becoming the first Archbishop of Canterbury in 601-604.

The mind has a peculiar habit of returning to happy memories and Clifford often recalled in his mind's eye the lovely Cathedral in Cairo, so light and airy, warm and welcoming. Yet, as he surveyed the magnificence of the building now in front of him he began to feel a sense of pride in the long history and heritage of the land of his birth and of the Christian Gospel that had reached out to many lands, including Egypt. He felt glad of his life, enriched by his wartime experiences: but here was home once more, and he felt a warm surge of enthusiasm as he entered that holy place, to explore the treasures within. Life was going to be good in Bristol, of that he felt confident - but just how good it was to become only time would reveal.

Moving to the city did not have many difficulties; he had lived in a hotel room whilst in Rugby and it was simply a matter of finding a similar haven in a suitable place. Clifton was fashionable, attractive, and most major streets were on a bus route directly down the hill to College Green and the Cathedral. A better arrangement could not have been envisaged and so Clifford found an amenable hotel, the Lansdown Hotel, in Pembroke Road,

Clifton, with kindly and welcoming hosts in **Mr. and Mrs. Henry Palmer**, an upstairs single room becoming 'home'. Thus installed, Bristol's newest resident felt ready for all that came his way. He remained at that address for many years, adding a few personal touches for his greater comfort. Often he would walk to the Cathedral for the day's work, returning home for a meal, retracing his steps for the evening's engagements.

But the route to the Cathedral was downhill; return after a busy day with a long uphill haul was not always attempted on foot. The bus was obviously the best method of return, and he could easily get one of the many which left the Centre to dispread themselves to all parts of northern Bristol via Whiteladies Road. However, there were many occasions over the years when he welcomed the offer of a friend whose car dropped him at his own front door. **Ron Apperley** was one such kindly gentleman, who lived in Clifton and who often transported Clifford home after Evensong in his later years. Mr. Apperley was one of the Cathedral's voluntary 'welcomers', and when on duty on Mondays would set out the chairs for the Special Choir rehearsal.

The bicycle? It had certainly accompanied Clifford on the train from Rugby but it probably never saw the light of day in Bristol until, after two years of dire neglect, it was pushed up Whiteladies Road to be sold!

Cathedral life was not unfamiliar to the new Organist; accustomed to the Newcastle and Cairo routines he quickly became acquainted with how things were done at Bristol.

The **Very Reverend Harry Blackburne** was his first **Dean**, followed by **Evered Lunt**, then **Douglas E.W. Harrison**, whom Clifford revered for his scholarship and wise counsel, and **Horace Dammers**, who helped to organise the Cathedral Choir's European Tour in 1981. Each one evoked great respect from Clifford and all of them supported and encouraged him. Whenever a Dean visited a choir rehearsal in Clifford's time, boys stood in respect and remained standing for the whole visit unless told otherwise, and Clifford, on these occasions, always referred to his visitor as "Mr. Dean".

The Cathedral's **Precentors** were the people with whom Clifford worked most closely, among whom were **Canon Evan Pilkington**, with whom he enjoyed a special warm relationship and rapport; **Canon David Isitt** with a fine musical background who, with Clifford, introduced the Easter Vigil, the Advent Service, and a form of Solemn Vespers on certain Sundays; **Canon Jim Free**, who became Precentor about eighteen months before Clifford's retirement. All his Precentors respected him for his care for every aspect of choral work with the Cathedral. They recognised his quality of life and the spirit with which he carried out his work. They found he had unfailing courtesy to all - young or old - and his gentle discipline of choristers meant that there were many who looked up to him then, and who always remembered him with respect and thankfulness. No-one could ever recall any occasion when he was absent or late, or when he lacked interest in his work.

Clifford's Precentors were amongst the first to realise his fondness for the 1662 Prayer Book, and that his love of music did not blind him to the importance of words. Indeed, the relation of music to words was, to Clifford, the ultimate vocal expression, whether prayers, hymns, Psalms or anthems.

The Precentors met with Clifford often, but once a week they met to choose hymns for the various services. Clifford was always a great inspiration at these times, which was valued. Canon Pilkington, in particular, had a marvellous relationship with him and shared Clifford's enthusiasm for music for almost seven years. He was always diplomatic concerning the music, though they saw eye to eye on most things. Nevertheless, he perpetually steered clear of choosing 'There is a green hill' because he well knew that Clifford regularly asked would-be choristers to sing a verse of this hymn during their auditions. (This fact was a constant source of amusement to generations of choristers.)

Canon Pilkington asserted that, to a parish priest, one of the hazards of life was his organist; in fact, he knew they could be a difficult body of men! But he worked with Clifford for seven years and found him "by far the highest powered and by far the easiest". He found a total openness and trust and true personal friendship.

Once settled at the Cathedral Clifford proved that he could, indeed, be completely loyal. Amongst all the many responsibilities that he carried, nothing was more important to him than his Cathedral work, the training of his choristers and lay clerks, and playing at Evensong. His own personal standards were quickly realised - his own deep faith became obvious from his words and actions and sustained him in all his work. But - he was no 'plaster saint' - he could (rarely) be very angry when really upset by something which to him was unwonted, and he could be caustic in his comments at times; in particular, he could not tolerate inappropriate or irreverent behaviour in others in the Cathedral, if ever he let slip an expletive it would be spoken with mock 16th century pronunciation "Bother-ay-see-on" but he remained a marvellous and influential example, as many were to realise in future years.

The Organist
The chief duties of the Organist and Master of the Choristers were to play each day for Evensong, services on Sundays, rehearse the choristers and lay clerks, and help in the planning of all services at the Cathedral, which also included playing on special occasions and at weddings and funerals.

Clifford's own dexterity as an organist received prominence, not only in voluntaries and postludes during regular services, but in regular recitals at lunch times, always giving immense pleasure with his wide-ranging repertoire to the many people who went to listen. He loved the instrument and it gave him great pleasure to create all the differing shades and tones that would reveal its capabilities with his own expertise.

His playing was inspiring to listen to and watch. His Sunday afternoon voluntaries were an institution - Bach, César Franck, and Vierne probably amongst his favourites. He could also realise orchestral scores on the organ in a colourful and totally convincing style. His quiet, extempore playing, especially before services, created a calm and reverent atmosphere in preparation for worship, and he would often 'introduce' the anthem by an improvised theme - an old Anglican tradition. At Christmastime, after the Bishop had spoken his good wishes for Christmas, Clifford would follow with a quiet Amen played on the solo manual.

He was utterly at home improvising, worshipping God at the console. In the music of the Cathedral and beyond his transparent love of God and devotion to Christ shone through.

He once told Chris Chivers that he grew up in anglo-catholic surroundings - he felt at home with that sort of churchmanship and in a way hankered after that kind of Christianity. Maybe his love of Elgar's **The Dream of Gerontius** came from the fact that it was his theology of the kingdom of heaven and of judgement. For a man so English, so rooted in Elgar and Vaughan Williams and the pastoralists, he delighted in Bach and Handel, but the modern continental composers - Dupré, Vierne, du Mage, to quote but a few - all helped him to express his emotions in music, for he was shy and retiring and reticent about himself.

He took part in the Communion Service, temporarily leaving the organ loft and, donning his academic gown, he would receive his bread and wine as unobtrusively as possible.

The Cathedral and its life became part of Clifford's very being, he was rarely away from his Cathedral, often refusing engagements further afield in favour of remaining to play for daily Choral Evensong . . . and it was not always playing to a packed congregation; the meagre congregation went into the choir seating, leaving the Nave dark and sombre. It never worried Clifford, however, he created the same worshipful atmosphere for the 'two or three gathered together' as he would do for a grand occasion. There was always a sprinkling of regulars which included a few female hopefuls and stalwart admirers who beamed cherubically and who were always given a wide berth at the close of the service.

He grew to love the building itself. One of his choristers, **Chris. Chivers**, remembered him with affection, had a lasting image of him, on a cold February afternoon, sitting at the back of the Cathedral, 'simply gazing at the vaulting'. He had a wonderful awareness of history and of the honour he felt at being a part of that. He really did understand and communicate what the 'beauty of holiness' could mean, especially in musical terms.

Clifford was essentially a cathedral organist of the old school, inheriting an exquisite style of **Psalm** playing and choral accompaniment from the tradition of **William Ellis**, **Charles Moody** and **Sir Edward Bairstow** in the north, and **Sir William Harris** of St. George's Chapel, Windsor. Clifford made his own selection of chants from two books used in alternate months, which included all the well known chants by Wesley, Stanford etc. He also wrote two chants specially for the Cathedral services.

He was a wonderful interpreter of the Psalms and his accompaniment was, in effect, 'orchestrated' (no other word) using the most imaginative combination of stops to colour the text. Many have not heard anything to equal it since, as he possessed a spirituality and a sensitivity to words which enabled him to express them in music.

Whilst chiefly traditionalist, Clifford did have an awareness of the direction in which the church was going and of his duty to respond to what the church required of him as a musician, but he felt justified in his insisting on using the late 17th and early 18th century settings of the **Canticles** - Kempton in B flat (the 5.15 at Kempton Park, as he used to call it!) and Kelway in A minor - settings way out of fashion but which Clifford understood to be quintessentially Anglican church music.

He was brought into the forefront of modern changes - the greatest change of all was the change of liturgy in the Eucharist, and in the Congregational Service. Under the guidance of Dean Douglas Harrison he was the first to introduce the new Series 2 in the 1960s. He was never really comfortable with many of the later modernisations of liturgical language. He simply found it less beautiful and less uplifting, and to ease the passage from the old to the new he wrote a congregational creed and a rather splendid ASB (Alternative Service Book) Eucharist (Kyrie, Gloria, Sanctus, Benedictus and Agnus) in B flat, which was used for a slide presentation on the new ASB across the Church of England in 1980, and which David Isitt co-ordinated with him. It was quite beautiful, highly effective, music, written for a choir and a building which he knew so intimately, and it added greatly to the preservation of the liturgy in Bristol. Regrettably, though, it never became more widely known. Always loyal to those with whom he worked, Clifford's acquiescence in the Series 2 owed much to the fact that Dean Harrison, whom he much admired, had a hand in the writing of it.

However, Clifford Harker had valid reasons for possibly appearing to be reactionary. He insisted that he was not against moving forward but felt strongly (as many others felt) that the new wording meant a losing of much of the language that was beautiful. For years, people had known the words such as the General Thanksgiving by heart - "We, Thine unworthy servants, do give Thee most humble and hearty thanks for all Thy goodness and loving kindness to us and to all men" - all those rolling phrases. The new version was in very basic English implying - "Thank you for feeding us" - which could never have such a profound effect on those in prayer. He was also disappointed at what had been done with some of the hymns. He considered it unpardonable that words of hymnwriters like George Herbert should have been altered and brought 'up to date', 'modernising' them, in effect. He had even heard on the radio 'updated' Collects by Cranmer which, to him, was absolutely monstrous. It was this kind of thing that went straight to his heart and just could not be borne. He knew he was being controversial but could only say how he felt, and he knew the Lord, at least, would understand.

At the same time, he found it sad that the wording in the original 1662 Prayer Book was not explained more to people, to help them understand what they were praying and, occasionally, he would encourage people to "go home and read the marvellous language of it". He thought the language had everything but wished the meaning of words had been better clarified. For instance, he wished that people were not put off by phrases like 'miserable sinners', because it meant 'sinners in need of mercy', that was all. It did not mean miserable in our sense, but 'in need of mercy' - like the miserichords in the choir - to have mercy on the old monks who could not stand through a service and were given something to rest upon. The translation of 'miserere nobis' was interesting in that it gave exactly the same rhythmic phrase as 'miserable sinners'. Clifford himself gloried in Cranmer's great litany, it was written in superb English, it was simple, and set to the dignified music of Tallis. He considered it 'a most glorious thing'.

Clifford gladly recognised the qualities of those with whom he worked. With Canon Evan Pilkington he worked on new pieces of liturgy, and a Good Friday Evensong with music and readings, an Advent Carol Procession, an Easter Day Evensong with Carols and Hymns in procession. With David Isitt, in the 1970s, he introduced an Easter Vigil and a form of Solemn Vespers on certain Sundays to replace Evensong. This last was a breadth of eastern and western orthodox chant together with that of the Anglican tradition, and it produced a creative and wonderful synthesis of different aspects of the Christian tradition.

Choir

Clifford was remembered with enormous affection by the many choristers who passed through the choir during his thirty-four years. He established a new tradition of music making, injecting a colossal amount of life into the singing of the choir and Cathedral worship in Bristol

Dr. Hubert Hunt had been distinguished as Organist and Master of the Choristers for forty-five years in the first half of the twentieth century followed, in post-war years, by **Alwyn Surplice** (1946-49). Clifford's arrival in Bristol, with his energy, dedication and (by now) vast experience, fostered a new era in the musical life, not only of the Cathedral, but in choral singing throughout Bristol (and, in time, Bath).

One of the great glories which the English church has retained is the fine expression of choral music, and Clifford was to become a legend in an uninterrupted tradition of excellence at Bristol. He embraced religious music from earliest roots to the most modern expression by contemporary composers. His method encompassed highly disciplined and articulate singing without compare.

Michael Doswell was Head Chorister when Clifford arrived to commence duties with the choir. Michael remembered the first time he saw him - "a rather imposing figure with a vigorous head of hair, dressed in a smart double-breasted suit, standing quietly in the Cathedral quadrangle waiting to be presented to his new choir. His slightly larger-than-life personality created an immediate impression but I little knew at the time what an enormous difference he was to be on me and, indeed, many others who came after me". Yes, countless boys were to experience the same first time - and lasting - impression of the new man.

A later chorister, **John Jenkins**, expressed similar sentiments - "I became a Cathedral chorister and fell under the influence of a man who was to make such an enormous impression on my life, and who still inspires me ..... as boys we learnt from him professionalism, the ability to work as part of a team and a duty always to give of our best".

Being a chorister was not just an aura of the popularly portrayed pink-cheeked angelic, with impeccably combed hair, frilled ruff, and who could soar to the top As with utter ease; once across the Rubicon life became a time of self discipline with a strict personal routine and, above all, boys just had to love singing.

In most cathedrals boys joined the choir at about seven or eight years whilst, in Bristol, boys normally joined at ten. On rare occasions it could be nine, the boys serving a probationer year by singing at weekends and in holiday periods until they entered the Cathedral School. Each year dozens of boys applied for the very few places available, and many were disappointed.

One such 'failure' was **Stephen Foulkes**, who applied about 1957. He recalled how he waited rather nervously in the Chapter House with dozens of other hopefuls before being summoned into the Music Room to be assessed by Mr. Harker. He was put at ease (though very much in awe of the choirmaster) and said he had prepared 'There is a green hill' to sing. After a short introduction two verses were sung, followed by a few aural tests, and the interview was over. (It is said that the choirmaster has, within the first few seconds, the answers to most of his questions about a prospective chorister.) Waiting back in the crowded Chapter House with his mother until everybody had been assessed, his was not amongst the names of successful candidates whose names were called out. Disappointing - but at ten it was not always a matter of life and death for the boy concerned, who realised he would not have to leave his good school friends after all. More often, parents were the ones to feel disappointment most and Clifford himself surely regretted many decisions which he was obliged to make at those times. Fortunately, love of singing prevailed and that particular candidate entered the choir in 1976 as a lay clerk, and was greatly valued for his fine bass voice.

Voice tests were similar for all boys. Strangely, most parents got to know what the required 'piece' should be as Mr. Harker always chose the same one. (And if Cecil Frances Alexander, the writer of 'There is a green hill', and William Horsley, the composer of the tune, only knew how well known the hymn would become to certain boys in the Bristol area, they would surely have been highly amused, to say the least!)

After a successful voice test the realities of the next few years began to sink in. There was, undeniably, much less free time than they had been used to. One important factor was the matter of school fees, and all boys were fortunate enough to be awarded a Choral Scholarship, when school fees were paid by the Dean and Chapter. Whilst the Cathedral School was a Direct Grant School, the terms of its tenure of the buildings was that the 'rent' was a free education to 18. When the School became independent and owned its buildings the Choral Scholarships was for 4 years only.

Once a boy was accepted for the choir he was usually a chorister until his voice 'broke'. This inevitable occurrence was always an unknown factor and was surely frustrating when a boy was singing at his best and thoroughly into his treble part. One famous treble, **Master Ernest Lough**, of Temple Choir, London, made his celebrated recording of 'Oh for the wings of a dove' when he was sixteen, though most boys' voices change several years earlier, but when a boy retired from the choir whilst in the transition period, another boy came in. A probationer was placed either on cantoris or on decani. After a probationary period he was permitted to put on the white surplice.

Note: Cantoris and Decani describe the north and south sides of the choir - Cantoris sat on the side with the Cantor (Precentor or Succentor), Decani sat on the side where the Dean was seated. By tradition, Decani sang 1st Choir and Cantors 2nd Choir. The boys were organised as follows (in order of seniority):

Cantoris 2 6 10 14 18 15 11 7 3
_____
Decani 1 5 9 13 17 16 12 8 4

'Moving up' generally included changing sides, although sometimes two boys would leave at the same time.

The number of choristers was normally eighteen, with a maximum of six probationers. It could happen, and sometimes did, that several boys' voices broke at almost the same time and took them out of the choir, thus probationer boys could find themselves suddenly catapulted along the row into regions of far more prominence. Realistically, boys could be probationers for some considerable time and moved up only when a vacancy occurred. Progression normally depended upon whenever Mr. Harker felt happy about it. Probationers did not process with the choir but sat, wearing cassock and ruff in the stalls between the choir stalls and the High Altar, arriving before the choir, and leaving afterwards. If there was enough music there would be a copy, otherwise there was only a psalter or hymn book.

Being made a full chorister was always formalised at a short service in the Chapter House before Evensong. At the induction a boy was invested by the Dean with a surplice, and prayers were said especially for him. This would be a proud moment for any serious-minded chorister. At this point, the boy's name would be placed at number 18 in Mr. Harker's black notebook (he would have been at the bottom of the page as a probationer). In this special book the life of every chorister would be noted; every promotion listed with details and dates, but also included was any misbehaviour - with the amount of 'fine' to be deducted from the payment made by the Chapter Clerk at regular intervals. Payments would be due for extra services and weddings and were real 'perks' for the time and effort put into the duties of choristers.

Misdemeanours were mostly a matter of waiting behind for Mr. Harker to appear from the organ loft after a service and for him to determine the severity of the offence on the evidence of the appropriate senior chorister, and ranging between sixpence and a shilling (or 2½ and 5p). Mr. Harker never used corporal punishment even when it was still applied by masters and prefects in the school. More major disciplinary problems were a matter of direct discussion between Mr. Harker, the school, and parents. Fortunately, serious problems rarely occurred and the boys loved him, calling him 'Cliff' out of earshot. On the other side of the coin, as it were, a Head Chorister could challenge a late or incorrectly dressed dean or other member of clergy, and if he could then recite correctly the Lord's Prayer in Latin he could claim half a crown from the erroneous clergyman.

To a large extent, choir discipline at services was the responsibility of 'corner boys', who sat at either end of the choir, and the Head Chorister. These were not chosen necessarily for academic or singing ability but were boys whom Mr. Harker found were responsible and dependable, and who could command respect from the other boys.

The duties of Head Chorister were not always to sing solo parts, but the honour carried with it certain disciplinary responsibilities, as well as keeping the pace by 'conducting' with his head. The greatest honour of all was to wear the coveted medal of office. By the time a chorister had graduated to become Head, in addition to the Cathedral Choir he would also be kept busy with studies as by then he would be working towards 'O' Level examinations, thus increasing the workload, but it was generally a happy period for him, and a memorable one, notwithstanding the opportunity of seeing Mr. Harker in a different context when the choir augmented the Special Choir in its Christmas and other concerts.

A chorister's weekday started at the Cathedral for 8.30 a.m. Practice, which meant a very early arrival at the bus stop for most boys. Even at that early hour, Mr. Harker appeared good humoured and genial, and could be quite witty, often greeting his boys with his favourite G&S quip "Me gallant crew, good morning!" The Choir Room, where chorister practices were held, also served as his office. (An adjacent room was used when the men were rehearsing with the choristers). This early Practice meant missing School Assembly and sometimes ate into the first few minutes of the first lesson. There was a great sigh of relief when morning practice was discontinued in 1959 or 1960, which helped the choristers to integrate more into the life of the school at that time of day. After school, at 4.0 p.m., there was 'free time' to put in some homework occasionally supervised by Mr. Harker as well as Choristers' Tea or, latterly, 40 minutes of practice before Evensong.

If any organisation is to function properly, it is dependent upon many activities that are carried on behind the scenes. One such vital function was Chorister Teas, and this was carried out by a rota of chorister mothers, who helped in various other ways, but this role in particular, was essential for the sustenance of the growing choristers between school and home, when Evensong was at 5.15 p.m., and boys could not arrive home until about 6.45 p.m. The ladies served Tea in the School Hall on Monday, Tuesday and Friday at the close of school, and provided tea, cakes and sandwiches to the boys. Mr. Harker also welcomed this chance to talk with choristers and their mothers and often partook of a jam tart with his tea. There was endless liaison between Cathedral and parents, often in preparation for choir events, notably when the choir left the precincts of the Cathedral to sing elsewhere, as they did occasionally. The chorister's life meant dedication, too, for parents, whose total support was paramount for the time that a boy remained in the choir.

On Wednesday sports afternoon at Golden Hill the boys needed to be back for 4.0 p.m. Evensong which was sung by the boys only. Occasionally the failure of the 145 bus to appear caused a late entrance for some of the choir! On Thursday afternoons there was neither school nor Evensong. School finished at 12 noon on Saturday, but Evensong was at 4.0 p.m., followed by full choir practice with the lay clerks. Sundays entailed two services - Morning Service at 10.00 a.m. and Choral Evensong at 3.30 p.m.

The **Lay Clerks** normally numbered six: two each of alto, tenor and bass, and one supernumerary of each voice joined the choir to sing at the weekends. These loyal gentlemen needed sympathetic employers as at least three days each week a prompt departure from work was necessary to get to Evensong in time. One lay clerk was not able to leave work until 5.0 p.m., and covered the journey on a bicycle, down the hill at high speed, and generally still buttoning his cassock as the choir processed into the Cathedral.

Choir Practice was usually in the Music Room, where Mr. Harker rehearsed the boys, using the special 'benches', a generous gift of the composer Sir Walford Davies, who was closely associated with the Cathedral in his later years. Generations of boys remembered those benches which were well used before and during Mr. Harker's time, and **Herbert Chappell**, an ex-chorister, vividly recalled them: "Choristers could half-stand, half-sit, such as you might find in French penal colonies in Sierra Leone, because you neither sat up straight, nor can you lounge and slouch". The idea was to give "lots of moral fibre and a top A flat occasionally". Herbert had become a chorister before Clifford arrived; he studied A level music with Clifford and had some organ tuition with him. He followed a career in music, having won a scholarship at Oxford through Mr. Harker's efforts with him, and at one time was well known as composer of the theme music for 'Songs of Praise' and the television serial 'The Pallisers'.

To choristers, choir practice was an education in itself. Mr. Harker's style was never to over-rehearse. The choir was his 'instrument', and boys learned musicianship with all its facets. Their training was to professional standards: they learned how to **listen** and to sing rhythmically, they learned the technique of 'placing' notes in the head, how to pitch a note and how to come in on a lead at the right pitch. Everyone who learned with Mr. Harker remembered his ability to play (or thump percussively) the piano so that the beat was as clear as his conducting.

Mr. Harker always spent at least one practice a week with the younger choristers, concentrating on breathing exercises and getting the tone he wanted. For breathing, this meant standing with the hands clasped behind the neck, and then pulling the elbows back with the intake of breath; this pulled up the diaphragm and opened the chest. There were scales - always descending so that the high tone from the head was emphasized - and arpeggio exercises with background harmonic accompaniment from senior choristers not involved. Mr. Harker looked after the boys' robes, making sure they were kept hung tidily, and he arranged for their laundering.

When getting ready for a service the choir assembled in the Cloisters and Mr. Harker always said a few words to the choir. If any boys fooled around he would **pretend** to be irritable and they recognised the caution, immediately curbing their high spirits. This was a measured practice as it ensured the boys were quiet and in control and so contrived a well ordered procession into the choir stalls.

In Cathedral services Mr. Harker was always loathe to do the 'modern' thing and direct the choir. He hated flamboyance in worship, directing only on Friday nights and at weekends (when there was unaccompanied music) and never for Psalm singing. When he did conduct it was minimal and in keeping with the reverent vein of the service. The boys found that this contrasted with their memories of Alwyn Surplice's great bird-like swooping movements. At chorister rehearsals Mr. Harker did sometimes conduct furiously and it was always a source of amazement to the boys how he could reach a great climax and yet get his hair back into place with a simple shake of the head.

Mr. Harker's music for the Cathedral choir was chosen with great care; as with all his choices he was conscious of the occasion, of the season, and strived to get the most suitable piece for everything that was planned. He was to influence the forming of the musical tastes of his boys at an early age. His obvious enthusiasm instilled in them a healthy appreciation of the cathedral repertoire - Stanford: Beati quorum via; Edgar Bainton (a former piano teacher of his): And I saw a new heaven; Brahms: How lovely are Thy dwellings; and the favourites - Schubert's The Lord is my Shepherd and Brother James' air.

But he was not afraid of modern music; he performed with the choir Britten's 'Jubilate', and gave the first performance of Geoffrey Bush's 'Missa Salisburiensis' (at which some cleric was known to mutter "Cats on the roof,

Clifford, cats on the roof!" At the same time, he was out of sympathy with musicology that he saw produced accurate, authentic, but soulless performances.

It was also true to say that unconsciously his choristers learned about training a choir, so that they came to apply his methods in their own circumstances. They learned how to achieve a balanced sound, how to deal with problems of diction and intonation.

The boys loved Mr. Harker and were amongst the best trained boys in the country. He always maintained that the over-controlled style practised by some choirs was inappropriate for the acoustic of Bristol Cathedral and the role of the choir in leading worship. He concentrated more on tone than the placing of final consonants (as they got lost, anyway). They received an outstanding musical education and were trained to professional standards in music as well as in personal self-discipline. There was growth in confidence and in time management, and an all-round training in real musicianship. If their musical interests did include the 'pop' aspect, it most certainly did not affect their choral singing style.

Some boys were prepared for Confirmation, making a personal commitment in the Christian life, and were confirmed at the School Confirmation Service in choir robes.

A number of Mr. Harker's choristers went on to pursue musical careers, particularly his organ students, and he remained interested in all they were doing, keeping in touch as they left for college or university, and encouraging them in every way. He displayed great pride in his former choristers, and generous in help over the checking of new compositions when asked to study them, making helpful suggestions about vocal lines, and shapes. He enjoyed going to see his boys conduct - as he did when **Chris. Chivers** was conducting Bach's St. John Passion for the first time during his time at Oxford. Mr. Harker liked to encourage and support his students in this way.

A positive and fair mentor, Mr. Harker inspired affection and loyalty from boys and lay clerks alike. He worked very hard and with utter devotion, and made it possible for boys to have instrumental tuition - a number of boys learning the organ under his direction - with the full support of **David Jewell**, who became Headmaster of the Cathedral School in 1970. Boys benefited from Mr. Harker's profound musicianship as well as his example as a fine Christian gentleman.

Chris. Chivers, in his memoirs of Mr. Harker, was generous in his praise of his former choirmaster. He said "I shall always remember what he taught me of God; his tremendous sense of humour - the wonderful shout of "fine 2p" which went up when some errant chorister was fined for some misdemeanour - Clifford almost self-mockingly knowing that even in 1977 two pence wasn't a lot of money; and the vividness of those drooping eyes, which sparkled in performance especially when at pianissimo the choir was 'brought off' and the piece closed with that characteristic right hand flick. It

23. Clifford and his 'boys'.

is indeed a rich legacy within which those of us who were his choristers locate ourselves."

How many choristers passed through Mr. Harker's hands it is difficult to estimate. Were the 'little black book' available it might reveal a realistic assessment but, in thirty-five years, assuming an average annual intake of six boys, this would indicate that about 200 boys were nurtured in their musical and devotional advancement. Without doubt, each would have his own memories. Particularly remembered would be the fine carol services at Easter, when carols were started first in the Cloisters then, as the choir moved to different parts of the Cathedral to sing, the organist would 'fill in' between verses until the choir was in the right place. The pattern was similar at Christmas, when the carols were sung in procession. The choir started at the far end of the cloisters, when the organ would start in G minor for the choir to sing Walford Davies' 'O filii et filiae'. They worked round the Cathedral from the Choir to the Lady Chapel, through the south transept by the night stairs, then along to the Christmas Tree, sometimes passing through the centre of the Nave to the Elder Lady Chapel (behind the organ) and back into the choir stalls. A carol was sung at each stopping point when the youngest chorister held Clifford's music. Sometimes the choir appeared on television during the Christmas Evensong. The boys were filmed in procession, and were excited later to see pictures of themselves on the front page of the Bristol Evening Post.

Memories would not all be of the Cathedral choir stalls; occasionally, the choir would sing elsewhere, and Bath Abbey was one place where Mr. Harker's choir was sometimes asked to sing Evensong. On these outings, the boys proudly considered themselves 'the professionals'.

The choir sang at some of the concerts given by the Special Choir. When that choir was first formed, the choristers sang the Soprano solos in Brahms' 'Requiem', sitting in their cassocks in the front of the Nave in a group immediately below Mr. Harker's rostrum, with the orchestra and choir behind. And, of course, the choristers always took part in the Carols and Christmas Music.

In 1978, when the choir sang in the Colston Hall at the Festival of Remembrance, during the two minutes' silence more than one boy noticed tears streaming down Mr. Harker's face. Undoubtedly, the war years always haunted his memories and were powerful ones for his formation as a person.

It was not all singing for the boys of the choir. Each year there was a treat for them in the form of a visit to the pantomime at the Hippodrome. A generous member of the Cathedral congregation always funded the outing and Mr. Harker preceded this by taking the boys out to tea at Carwardine's Café in Baldwin Street. In fact, it is said that Mr. Harker once wrote music for one of the Bristol pantomimes at the Old Vic. and, if that is true, then it would most certainly have been full of tremendous wit and fun.

There was a performance of Gilbert and Sullivan's 'Trial by Jury' given, with orchestration under the confident baton of Mr. Harker. It was a single performance in the YMCA Theatre as a Cathedral School concert, directed by Rev. John (Oscar) Rankin, the Succentor. Some of the choristers were involved as the Bridesmaids (!), the more senior choristers acting as members of the public gallery. One chorister was bribed to play the jilted bride, Angelina, (without, apparently, any lasting effect upon his reputation then or at any time). It was all tremendous fun as well as hard work, and probably the only time when Mr. Harker conducted a School performance. Michael Dyer and his parents were instrumental in promoting the production as, indeed, they were key players (with the Headmaster, Cecil G. Rich) in getting together ex-choristers and other musicians in the Cathedral School, both pupils and teachers, to form a School Choir to enhance School worship in the Cathedral. Further, these opportunities nurtured the musical abilities in the boys which resulted in a number of them going into vocations associated with their musical interests.

It was not all music, by any means; the choristers looked forward to their annual cricket match against the Lay Clerks. It is difficult to imagine a team of eighteen or so taking on another team of six or so, but it seemed to work out well, age and experience balancing youth and quantity. It was always a time of terrific fun when the two teams strode out of the pavilion at Golden Hill. Mr. Harker was there, of course, jovial and supportive, looking quite dashing, and uncharacteristic, in his yellow pullover (all the rage in the fifties days and admired by the boys), smoking the occasional Churchman Tipped cigarette (was no other make relevant?).

From 1981 the choir began to make Summer Tours in European countries. This was to be a holiday eagerly anticipated by those involved. The Tours will be described more fully in Chapter 7.

Mr. Harker's concern for his boys was almost like that of a father. **Geoffrey Hudd**, a chorister of the 1950s regarded him, alongside his own father, as one of the major mentors of his development as a person. Mr. Harker's concern was such that if a boy was ill or in hospital he would visit and keep in touch until the boy's recovery was complete.

As boys left the choir many remained in contact with the Cathedral, joining a rota to provide Servers and Crucifers for Sunday services. The Dean used to meet them to keep them together socially and occasionally an outing was arranged. They always asked for their number to include Mr. Harker and, naturally, he was happy to join in such functions.

Good friendships were formed during chorister years and it was inevitable that many boys joined the **Bristol Cathedral Old Choristers' Association** (formed in 1919), to which choristers of many generations had belonged. The Association was very active between the wars but lapsed in the early fifties, being kept going by a few loyal members. At Clifford's 25th Anniversary in 1977 at the Cathedral many previous choristers were present, resulting in renewed life for the organisation and it thrived for the next ten years. During that time there were reunion dinners and many social functions; a flourishing old chorister choir (known as Collegium Choristarum) sang under Dr. John Craig, singing Compline at Advent and Lent and opportunities to re-constitute the choir were constantly sought after he moved through his medical work in 1983.

The Old Choristers' Association was engaged in fund raising activities to help defray the cost of the Choir Tour in 1981.

When the Cathedral School became independent in 1975 the matter of choristers' school fees was one of the problems. Therefore, a **Choral Foundation** was set in motion. The foundation committee comprised Peter Bale (Chairman), Anthony Bailey (Secretary), Douglas Woods (Hon. Treasurer), Clifford Harker, Canon Evan Pilkington (Chapter representative), David Cannock (Chorister parent) and Gerry Nichols (past chorister). Bursaries were made available through the Foundation, which was sustained financially through Cathedral grants and various forms of fund raising.

The aims of the Foundation were to support the English Choral tradition in Bristol Cathedral, and to assist in the education of choristers by the funding of bursaries, thus helping to preserve the choral tradition and musical excellence dating back to the foundation of the Cathedral in 1542. The Choral Foundation was a tangible link with the musical history of Bristol Cathedral, with its former organists Edward Gibbons (brother of Orlando Gibbons) and Elway Bevin (a pupil of Thomas Tallis). There was a succession of thirty-two Organists and Masters of Choristers who ensured that 'the praise of God shall day by day be sung with perpetual jubilation'.

Organ Students

For a considerable time Clifford had no assistance, but as work developed it became expedient that some form of help would be of great advantage. Teaching music and piano had not been his first love, but teaching the organ was altogether different for him. He found his organ students to be seriously interested in their chosen instrument; therefore, he enjoyed a subsidiary (but infinitely related) occupation giving organ tuition to several students, some of whom were choristers, and in time one or two progressed sufficiently to assist him at services, eventually themselves becoming accomplished organists, fitted for sharing the duties in an official capacity. This careful nurturing was more than rewarding for Clifford, who recognised much potential in his students, and in time he felt fully confident in his Assistants, knowing they would contribute significant dignification whenever they played at services. In fact, an Assistant was to become Clifford's right hand man and essential to Cathedral music, though each one in turn found themselves privileged indeed to be afforded this prerogative.

For their part, students came to realise the great advantages they enjoyed through studying with such a tutor. Clifford was a meticulous teacher, kind but firm, and generous in the extreme once he found his students to be fully committed. When giving a lesson he would encourage his pupil with "capital" or "that goes well now". He inspired them and enabled them to reach beyond themselves, his influence helping them (as countless others were to echo) to appreciate the extraordinary richness of music and a love of beauty which enabled them to become better people.

Michael Doswell (Head Chorister when Clifford arrived) was Clifford's first Pupil Assistant in the early 1950s. He discovered that he had been given poor grounding in the organ previously, but through Clifford's kindness and perseverance faults in his playing were gradually ironed out. As Michael's organ skills developed, Clifford eventually invited him to be his Pupil Assistant. This entailed being present at all sung services in order to turn the pages for him, and to pull out the occasional stop when Clifford's hands were full in busy passages of music. Michael recalled that sitting in the organ loft and watching Clifford play, so effortlessly, was in itself an education, but being taught by Clifford was something else. Clifford helped him to realise his own potential. Other duties involved playing for the Sunday afternoon service, on miscellaneous occasions such as Confirmations, and providing half an hour of music before the concerts given by the Cathedral Special Choir, of which he also became a member. Sometimes a request for music came from outside the Cathedral, such as a recital or, as once happened to Michael, a Gang Show(!).

Michael returned to help Clifford for a time, following his absence on National Service.

Clifford's complete dedication to his work inevitably meant that he rarely missed a service; once playing Evensong during Michael Doswell's time he played with his arm in a sling, having sprained his wrist in a fall - nobody would have guessed.

Occasionally, Assistants were invited to dinner with Clifford at a favourite restaurant in those days - Horts in Small Street. He entertained with his own reminiscences of experiences in Cairo, his time in Rugby, perhaps sometimes discussing proceedings of a recent Cathedral Organists' conference, and was altogether the genial host, speaking as if the listener knew all the people who came into the conversation.

Most Assistants' experiences were of a similar nature, though, naturally, each had his own particular tale to tell, although Michael Doswell's gratitude to Clifford was so overwhelming that in 1953 he dedicated one of his own first compositions, an anthem 'Lead us, O Father' (words by Burley), to 'Clifford Harker and the Choir of Bristol Cathedral'.

Particularly enjoyable occasions for a number of years were the religious plays given in the Cathedral by the **Guild of Cathedral Players**. These pageants were produced by **Freda Hulcoop** supported by her husband, Ernest. Freda taught at the Cathedral School and helped Teddy Martin with the school plays. In 1945 the Cathedral School produced its school play in the Cathedral - 'Murder in the Cathedral' - which was well received, and in 1947 the Guild was inaugurated to present suitable plays in the Cathedral with the motto 'Worship through Art'

Robert Peters, a keen member of the Guild throughout its existence, has his own memories. 'When Clifford arrived at the Cathedral he soon became a very close collaborator and contributed much to the work of the Guild. He provided music on every occasion and if nothing appropriate was available, he wrote it.

'Religious drama in churches was in its infancy at that time and the plays attracted interest and support. After plays were performed in the Cathedral the Guild began to take the production to parish churches throughout the diocese and beyond. One notable 'first' was a presentation of 'In Three Days', an Easter play, performed in Horfield Prison. After that, Leyhill Open Prison came on to the circuit and plays there became a regular feature. This started the practice of inviting parties of the inmates to visit the Cathedral where they were entertained to tea. Clifford was closely involved in all this.

'There was another production of 'Murder in the Cathedral' and another title was 'Our Lady's Tumbler', by Ronald Duncan. Clifford played the musical brother in the monastery and wrote the anthem which he directed on stage.

'He was a dear and greatly valued friend and member until the Guild finally dissolved in the 1980s'.

Assistants were involved by providing appropriate organ interjection during the play, thus heightening the dramatic effect. Clifford was responsible for the musical direction, conducting the choir who sat behind in the Lady Chapel, and even taking part once as a Bishop in 'Our Lady's Tumbler'!

A number of amusing incidents occurred at these times, for ever imprinted on Assistants' minds. **Michael Doswell** was required to fill in with improvised music at certain points during the action. He remembered with much mirth one rehearsal: - "I never ever saw Clifford laugh quite so much as on one occasion I heard the words "Now, some music now" urgently coming from the floor of the Nave. Unfortunately, I was unable to gather my wits sufficiently to provide something appropriate, and played the first thing that came into my head, which was the opening bars of 'Rule Britannia' .... and this in the middle of 'Murder in the Cathedral'."

Clifford composed the music for 'the indefatigable Freda', whose personality was larger-than-life, but who was an extremely good producer. The Hulcoops, together with Mr. and Mrs. Graham Hooper, occupied a prominent place in Clifford's social life for a number of years and were very good friends of his. Freda often exchanged flippancies with Clifford and once asked him if he liked her new hat. He replied, with a wicked smile "What do you call that, your Edgar Allan?" (giggles all round)

Lionel Pike was Clifford's Pupil Assistant for two years from 1957 to 1959, and also played when the plays were performed. He also helped with 'Murder in the Cathedral'. During this play, amongst his responsibilities was the task of adding dramatic effect at the point when Thomas à Becket was struck down by soldiers. He was amazed at the tremendous result achieved when Clifford had explained how it should be done by placing his hands on as many notes as possible to produce three deafening blasts whenever a sword struck home.

As Assistant, Lionel would sometimes need to practise on the organ late in the evening and would have to go to the Cathedral when it was not in use and unlit. The only light switch was in the transept and the organ was approached by this small light only, after the organ key had been located. There was a tale that the ghost of a Black Canon walked across the south transept and once he was frightened by a noise, but the footsteps coming from the Dean's room was only a hale and hearty Clifford, so all was well. Other people reported 'ghostly happenings' from time to time, which could be just as satisfactorily explained.

Perhaps more amazing would be the times when, on big occasions, Lionel had to take over the organ from Clifford. They would change places during a period of improvisation without the slightest change in playing being detected. It was a clever manoeuvre used by Clifford and his Assistant at many such times.

A number of 'behind the scenes' ploys were used in order not to disturb the smooth running of a service, and **Gerry Nichols**, who was a chorister in the early Sixties, very often asked Clifford if he might join him and **Michael Dyer** in the organ loft. He remembered that it was sometimes necessary to give the note (or a chord) for an unaccompanied item and this was most often done with the organ. Clifford did own a pitch pipe with a rotating scale to indicate the varied pitch. Why he could not set the pipe beforehand, or do it in a relaxed manner, was always a mystery, but whenever he tried to use it Clifford, with closely knit brow, kept the choir in silence and the service suspended whilst he tried to select the right note. After many frustrations, it was felt that a quiet chord on the organ was a more satisfactory method of avoiding such an embarrassing hiatus. That was another endearing facet of Clifford.

Gerry, who often enjoyed the privilege of turning over the pages for Michael at Special Choir (and Bristol Choral Society) concerts, very quickly observed the musical relationship between Clifford and Michael Dyer. At close quarters there was certainly a degree of telepathy involved. When using the organ to accompany Special Choir concerts it was necessary to play the organ about half a beat ahead of the arm movements of Clifford to make it sound right in the Nave. At that time there was no closed circuit television and so the organist had to look over his left shoulder to watch and anticipate the beat whilst playing with both hands and feet!

Another diversion was to improvise voluntaries after Cathedral services using the chamber organ in the Eastern Lady Chapel. Clifford would play the small organ and Michael the main organ: no holds (or key changes) barred!

Michael Dyer was Clifford's Assistant for a number of years and they shared a special relationship. He was Clifford's right hand man and there was close relationship with Michael and his family. It was a severe shock to Clifford when he learned of Michael's untimely death in 1973. He said he felt as though part of him had been cut off. He treasured greatly a gift that Michael made to him: it was a wooden case, carefully and skilfully crafted to contain two conducting batons, and this remained a constant reminder of his friend and companion.

Another promising organ student, **David Moon**, who assisted Clifford when John Jenkins (who followed Michael Dyer) was away at Durham University, also died at the age of seventeen years, at the very outset of his promising career, and much missed by his tutor.

Sitting in the organ loft gave these young men a feeling of elation in more than one sense. **Chris Chivers** remembered how he would watch Clifford **pray** the Psalms through the immense sensitivity of his accompaniment to them. Clifford probably found it difficult to express his emotions except through his playing. Chris., like many others, experienced the pleasure of seeing Clifford's enjoyment of organ playing in hymns like 'Ye watchers and ye holy ones' to the tune *Lasst uns erfreuen*, and his great fervour when he came to the last verse of 'Allelujah, sing to Jesus' to *Hyfrydol*, when he got very emotionally involved - a canon at the top in the second half, and an Elgarian climax using the very top of the keyboard. Many organ students were to remember moments such as these.

Another organ scholar, **Stephen Taylor**, was often in the organ loft when Clifford played for services and has lasting memories of his remarkable accompanying of the choir especially in the Psalms. The Cathedral organ is in an awkward position for accompaniment of the congregation in the nave, and Clifford had two ways of bringing out the tune - either by playing the tune up octaves in the right hand, or by playing both hands an octave higher with a manual 16-foot stop added. On that particular type of organ both were excellent solutions, and served to stand Stephen himself in good stead in similar circumstances.

One last Evensong before a summer holiday Clifford was leaving immediately for a destination in Switzerland. He was tied for time to get away, so in the organ loft was his suitcase - placed there ready to pick up as he slipped away after the anthem, whilst Stephen was left to play the final voluntary.

Stephen Taylor became a chorister in 1960. His brother, Richard was Head Chorister around the same time, and the two boys took part in the performance of 'Trial by Jury', experiencing what it was like to be 'bridesmaids' for an evening! However, it did not leave any permanent mark upon their young career as Stephen became an organ pupil (1963-4) eventually following a career in music.

The whole Taylor family was thoroughly involved in Cathedral activities for the whole of the time that the sons were choristers; Mrs. Taylor was a willing and loyal provider of choir teas.

Clifford was also aware of his Cathedral congregations, however, and would often play a thrilling piece at the end of a service, the Widor

'Toccata in F' being one such favourite. He would look over the edge of the organ loft at the end of the music and see an unusually large collection of people who had been listening, and he would invariably say, very tongue in cheek, and imitating the Bristol accent "They only stay for the *Toccatuls*".

Holiday times were when Clifford could share his duties with his assistants. On Good Fridays, when there was the Three Hours' Devotion, **Lionel Pike** received what Clifford assumed "a fair division of labour" - Lionel playing 12 till 2pm, whilst Clifford did 2 - 3pm.

There were some special precautions to be observed in Lent. Every Ash Wednesday the Assistant was instructed: "We mustn't use the Tuba in Lent". (Too raucous, perhaps?) Tubas had a habit of making unwonted entry: Clifford was fond of telling his Assistants about the time when he had played an Amen on the Tuba, quite in error, at the end of Midnight Mass, thinking he was on the soft strings, when the Bishop liked a quiet Amen after the Blessing. Therefore, a word of caution to young organists: "Never leave a Tuba lying around".

Care with organ stops was always vital, and Clifford once confided to Lionel a very embarrassing experience he had had during his student days. Messiah was being performed in the Royal Albert Hall, with its mighty organ, and Clifford was the student playing for Sir Malcolm Sargent. During the rehearsal the choir reached almost the end of the Hallelujah Chorus, where there come five Hallelujahs, four of which have a quaver rest between, the last one having two quavers rest. At this point, Sargent stopped and complained to Clifford that the organ was not loud enough. "Add the full Great, and add a Tuba." Again, "Harker, I can't hear the organ, add another one." Then "Add all the Tubas .....thank you, do that tonight." When playing at the concert Clifford, trying hard to get all the stops pulled out, miscounted, and came down full hard during the rest ..... thereafter, whenever his organists and choristers had this chorus to perform, they were **thoroughly** drilled to count: "Hallelujah (one), Hallelujah (two), Hallelujah (three), Hallelujah (four, and no more) before the final one.

Most of Clifford's Assistants went on to pursue careers in music in one sphere or another - **Lionel Pike** and **Stephen Taylor** won scholarships to Oxford, **David Wookey** went to Cambridge, **Michael Doswell** became a music teacher, **Michael Pain** went on to teach music and organ and became a church organist. Many choristers, too, were to follow a musical career, all retaining a great love of music as a result of Clifford's grounding. **Chris. Chivers** was eventually to become Canon Precentor (as Clifford always said he would) at St. George's Cathedral, Cape Town. **Gerry Nichols**, together with many others, found fulfilment in being surrounded by music making as a lifetime pleasure. Clifford was known to advise each one: "Don't expect musical opportunities to fall into your lap - you have to create them." Good advice to serve them well in building a career. They constantly felt his influence, often thinking back to the time when privileged to work with

Clifford and, especially when faced with a problem in some musical situation found, in the recesses of their memory, a solution.

Of all Clifford's Assistants, one was to become a lifelong close friend. This was **John Jenkins**. He was an organ pupil and still at the Cathedral School when Michael Dyer died. Clifford brought John in at very short notice to help him, obviously knowing that he was capable of undertaking the demands to be laid upon him. Used to Cathedral life already, as he had been a chorister, John took on Assistant's duties with terrified excitement and he gradually became proficient in his new duties. However, the work also included accompanying Clifford's choral societies and John felt very much 'dropped in at the deep end', finding the rehearsing of works like Verdi 'Requiem' an altogether new and terrifying experience as he started to accompany the Special Choir during their rehearsals of this work. But the kindly and understanding conductor gave him tips on how to cut corners with the accompaniment, which helped him to become more eased and, eventually, to enjoy the rehearsals. John continued in this capacity for some time before finally leaving Bristol for university and a subsequent career in music. Clifford remained grateful and indebted to John for his willingness to step in at the emergency and they became close friends. John's parents were also good friends of Clifford's and he spent time at their home, including Christmas, for many years. For his part, Clifford was delighted to watch John's progress and encouraged him in every way; even dedicating one of his organ compositions to John.

As Clifford retired and eventually became less active, it was John (with a few close friends, some of whom were Aileen and Robert Moon, Mr and Mrs Norman Gough, and Mary Sheppard) who helped him with his affairs and thus was able in some way to repay what he felt he owed his good friend.

Martin Schellenberg became Clifford's Assistant when John left the area to teach. In addition to Assistants, Clifford had a few organ pupils from time to time. These were not attached to the Cathedral, and Clifford managed to fit in lessons during quiet times at the Cathedral, around 10.30 to 11 am. There would be organ tuition and Theory lessons in preparation for external examinations. In the 1950s, one of his pupils was **Marion Parsons**, who had already received organ tuition before taking more advanced examinations. A senior pupil at the Collegiate School, Winterbourne, she had organ lessons with **Miss Enid Hunt** (daughter of Dr. Hubert Hunt), walking to nearby Winterbourne Church with Miss Hunt and another girl who would act as 'organ blower' during the lesson. When preparing for an examination, Clifford would take her across College Green to play the organ of the Lord Mayor's Chapel where the eventual examination would take place. Marion sometimes had an opportunity to sit in the organ loft during Evensong, which gave her ideal instruction in accompaniment for services.

Michael Pain, too, was an organ pupil. He was given a scholarship by the Cathedral School to have lessons with Clifford (1969-71). He also helped with rehearsal accompaniment with the Cathedral Special Choir and Bristol Choral Society, once sub-conducting in Holst's 'Hymn of Jesus', and played the organ at some of the performances of the Guild of Cathedral Players.

Other local organ students were prepared for advanced examinations, such as FRCO, were **Ray Hillman**, **Gary Desmond** and **Christopher Cox**.

School Classes

Clifford loved talking about music. In the 1960s he used to go by train on Thursdays to teach at a girls' school in Corsham. Occasionally, he gave lessons in Music Appreciation to classes at the Cathedral School, illustrating Programme Music with examples from works such as Smetana's 'Vltava' and Beethoven's 'Pastoral Symphony', and at some time he taught 'A' Level Theory to pupils at the school. Many people, including his choirs, were to remember how he would sit at the piano and explain just how a piece of music worked. He liked to illustrate how good a composer Sir Arthur Sullivan was in his orchestration - this was during summer rehearsals for a G&S concert.

In the past, churches and cathedrals were used strictly for worship but in the twentieth century a more broad-minded approach gradually opened Bristol Cathedral to embrace more public events, and the Cathedral Organist was frequently involved.

Broadcast services and organ recitals were made on the radio, and special occasions were covered by the BBC also. With the advent of television it was a delightful discovery for many 'viewers' to be taken into the Cathedral to share Christmas services and other occasions in the church year - all from the comfort of their own armchair. Joking aside, television was indeed a godsend to people confined within their own home and to hospitals and institutions; when those unable to attend worship could share it through this medium.

There were occasions when the BBC West of England Orchestra broadcast recitals from the Cathedral, many of these players also playing in Clifford's concerts in the Cathedral and elsewhere, and **Reginald Redman**, Director of the BBC West of England Singers, gave concerts with his choir and recitals and concerts with the Cathedral Choir. Clifford appreciated the skills of Redman. Once, just as a broadcast service was about to begin Clifford, already keyed up, lost his temper momentarily with the choristers (who, no doubt, were equally excited). He told Lionel Pike, then Head Chorister, in a whisper, that he remembered Reginald Redman's complete composure in a similar situation and regretted his own lack of control.

The Film

In 1978, the Cathedral Authorities were approached by a film company to shoot part of a film within the Cathedral building. Permission was granted and although the plot was extremely bizarre it made life interesting and somewhat more colourful for those included whilst the filming period lasted. It was *'The Medusa Touch'*, starring Richard Burton (famous for his Shakespearean roles and for being one of several husbands of a well known glamorous American film star). The protagonist had powers to make disasters happen and at one point the film showed the Cathedral walls crumbling and crashing down, whilst the invincible organist, (Clifford in a brief moment of glory), continued to play surrounded by falling masonry. Such are the skills of film makers! Clifford made a wonderful and natural actor in this episode.

Other shots of the film were made in the locality and the choir, who had also made their film debut, were encouraged to become extras. The experience was fun for those who took part but when borrowed cassocks were returned, which had been loaned to film company actors, they were found to be in a sorry state, and although the Dean and Chapter were paid for the privilege by the film company, no-one at the Cathedral was best pleased.

Clifford, of course, bore it all with quiet martyrdom and whenever the subject of the film was raised afterwards, he would refer to it as "a dreadful film". He saw it once only and found the hospital scenes gruesome, but he was paid the handsome sum of £90, which amused him because he felt he had contributed so little.

Pageantry and Ceremonial

Life at any cathedral includes many special events and Bristol was no exception. There were the annual commemorative services of numerous organisations: Bristol University Beginning of Term Services were held in the Cathedral and for many years Clifford was organist on these occasions. After the Bristol Polytechnic was founded, eventually becoming the University of the West of England, all their degree ceremonies were held at the Cathedral, as were those of several theological colleges in the city.

One privilege of Bristol is to have a Lord Mayor, the annual mayor-making ceremony being held in May, and this ceremony is held in the unique Lord Mayor's Chapel. Nevertheless, the Lord Mayor attended many official functions at the Cathedral in Clifford's period, symbolising the city's civic life in its multitude of forms, not least a visit of **Her Majesty the Queen** in 1973, at the City's 600th celebration of its Charter as City and County.

Clifford loved the pageantry associated with this occasion; it made him feel very proud to be involved and he worked hard to ensure that everything was done properly. Everyone at the Cathedral ensured that things were in truth 'shipshape and Bristol fashion', and Clifford, high churchman that he was, liked things done in great style. He, as much as anyone else, realised the tremendous honour made to the City by this visit. Little did he realise that a good number of years later he would again meet his Queen in the place he loved most.

The Annual Civic Service was another sparkling event, with the Lord Mayor, Aldermen, and Police representatives striding up the Nave with their maces.

Bishops, too, from other dioceses would visit, when pomp abounded, sometimes even on Christmas Morning. The Merchant Venturers went to the Cathedral for their Annual Charter Day Service after which boys and girls were given the traditional Colston's buns, and several local independent schools, including Colston's Boys' School, Colston's Girls' School, and Red Maids School, all held their annual Commemoration Services there.

Weddings, too, were held occasionally at the Cathedral, often requiring the singing of the choristers. Some of these were especially happy occasions for Clifford when it happened to be the wedding of an ex-chorister. For these, Clifford was always more than happy to help plan the music for the ceremony, as he did for **Stephen and Penny Parsons**, and to do his part in making the service an extra special and memorable occasion for them.

Diocesan Festivals

The annual Diocesan Choral Festivals took place at the Cathedral in late September or in October. This was a long-standing event and choirs throughout the whole of the Bristol Diocese were invited to sing specially rehearsed music at Choral Evensong on Saturday afternoon, and was a broadening experience for many small church choirs who appreciated the chance to sing more ambitious music with a larger number of people.

The music for the service was decided by a committee of representatives from the Diocese, put together in book form, and distributed after Easter so that choirs could spend the summer learning. There were four hymns (mostly well known), two anthems, a setting of the Magnificat and Nunc Dimittis, responses, a Psalm, to be prepared.

During the rehearsing period Clifford would have time to visit some choirs, by invitation, and put them through their paces. This extra tuition from The Conductor was always welcomed, though it was not possible for him to visit all choirs taking part. His influence, his calmness and good humour in these circumstances was felt then, as a number of boys in local choirs later became part of the Cathedral choir.

When the great day finally arrived choirs would assemble in the Cathedral for rehearsals; people from outlying areas travelling into Bristol in a specially hired coach.

Kathleen Hillier, whose choir was in the Malmesbury deanery, had very vivid and happy memories of the occasions in Clifford's time: "All our collars and robes had been carefully washed and pressed and we were excited at finding our robing area, either in the Cathedral itself or in the Cathedral School. They were left there during the rehearsal, 2-4pm. The Choirs spread across the transept in front of the choir stalls and back into the nave, the sound of the organ coming from behind us. Therefore, Clifford on the rostrum was ever imploring us to watch the beat, sing with the baton, raging, cajoling, flailing arms, immense energy, ever inspiring, bringing out the best in us. What with the time lag and our inexperience it must have been very hard work indeed.

There was just enough time after the rehearsal to take our sandwiches to the seats or grass on College Green before we were robed, waiting in the cloister yard, taking delight in all the different colours and shapes of the robes - a motley throng.

The processional Cross led the way through the West Door and all we'd practised came to fruition plus the highlight of an anthem sung by the Cathedral Choir. There would be an address by someone well known and well geared to the needs of choristers.

It was a satisfying occasion. The bus took us home, stopping at Chipping Sodbury for fish and chips! A real red letter day."

Some of Clifford's music was sung at the Festivals, in 1957-58 'O God of Bethel' was sung to a tune founded on the Scottish Tune **Strathcaro**, and in 1976 he wrote a Laudate Dominum for Chorus, Brass and Timpani, which the choir found tremendously exciting to sing.

Kathleen found singing in the Cathedral so enjoyable that she belonged to the Special Choir for many years, and used her musical talents to the full, being organist at her church, Holy Cross in Sherston for many more years, including Clifford's organ pieces very often in her repertoire.

After Clifford's retirement this event in time became the responsibility of the Royal School of Church Music, who organised similar days of choral music but was opened to choirs of all denominations.

1971 brought a newcomer to the Cathedral who was to make quite an impact, especially on the musical life there. **Rex Hipple** was appointed Sub-Sacristan and Head Verger, having previously worked with the BBC for thirty years. At once he noticed Clifford's charm and enormous solid expertise.

The two men got on very well indeed and always had an extremely good relationship. Rex brought with him extensive recording and amplification expertise, which would be beneficial to worshippers and clergy alike. Perhaps Clifford was a little concerned and wary of any intrusion of technology into his way of life. He was no fan of recorded music and did not possess a music system or hi-fi, or anything mechanical beyond a straightforward radio and a tape recorder given him about 1960 (which he used to listen to recordings made by Thomas Beecham and John Barbirolli). His friends could not imagine how he managed to survive all those years, but one suspects that his early training in listening always held good and he, not being adept with 'bally machines', was happy to be as he had always been.

He had a patient 'steersman' in Rex, however and was at first reluctant to record but, little by little, he was nurtured into the mysteries of the recording machine, eventually discovering that so long as someone else's

24. Bristol Cathedral Choir, Clifford conducting.

finger was on the button it was not nearly so painful after all. Had it not been for the sympathetic patience of Rex Hipple, Clifford would never have been persuaded to produce those atmospheric recordings of music in the Cathedral that were a great triumph; Carols and Christmas music being amongst his most meritorious successes. He did not really understand tape recorders and his famous utterance "Oh, how I loathe machines" caused quite a stir at more than one recording session. It really did require composure on all sides.

Clifford adapted to recording and gradually began to listen to tapes which Rex had made in the Cathedral and in time actually admitted that he rather enjoyed re-living high moments in performances. It is certain that if Clifford had to live on a desert island he would definitely not have wanted to be without a recording of the Special Choir Carol evenings, particularly of 'Good King Wenceslas' and 'The Holly and the Ivy', with their own brilliantly sparkling orchestration arr.C.H.

Rex Hipple's amazing achievements in guiding Clifford through four recordings of music at the Cathedral was outstandingly commendable, and enabled the Master and his music to be heard all over the world.

There was one brief piece on tape which Clifford was glad could be 'wiped off', however. His singing was known to be diabolical (and prevented at all costs). One recording was made which demonstrated Clifford 'baying' in a most unmusical voice whilst beating time on the music desk. Immediate First Aid editing was employed, to everyone's great relief.

It is probably true that there are statutes for most Cathedral choirs which state that the Master of Choristers must be capable of taking his place at the appropriate voice in the cathedral choir if necessary. Someone jokingly said once that they were not certain anyone read that when Clifford was appointed, but noted with great relief that had singing been stipulated when Clifford had applied for Bristol how much the poorer thousands of people would have been.

There was only one occasion when Rex found himself at cross-purposes with Clifford's opinion. There was a time when the Cathedral bells became very popular and many groups came to ring, some peals lasting three hours or so. Nerves stretched to breaking point in the Hipple household, who lived very close to the Cathedral, and Rex asked the Committee if the amount of playing could be controlled, but Clifford felt that the bells were part of the music of the Cathedral. Perfectly right, of course, but **he** was not trying to get three young children to sleep during those evenings. This was one of the very few differences between the two men, and they remained very good friends to the last.

There was no slowness on the part of the Cathedral authorities to pay tribute to Clifford's service. On 21st September, 1974, the occasion of his 'Silver Jubilee' was celebrated with a dinner to which a goodly number of his past and present associates were invited. Much complementary preparation had been made in readiness for the grand occasion, some in secret, which was to give Clifford pleasant surprises at the event, and a lot of the planning was done by **Mary Sheppard**, a good friend who worked tirelessly in both Cathedral Special Choir and Bristol Choral Society. Mary was also involved in preparations for Clifford's eventual Retirement Dinner.

After a Reception and lavish Dinner, and the formalities of the Loyal Toast and Dean's Remarks had passed, the **Reverend Canon Evan Pilkington** introduced tributes to Clifford's work and music. On this occasion Rex Hipple was there to make cassette recordings of the evening, but many discreet enquiries had been taking place beforehand and tapes were played which brought greetings from a number of friends from Clifford's life before Bristol. First were voices from some friends in **Newcastle**, followed by the **Reverend Arthur Burrell's** voice which brought back memories of wartime Egypt, Cairo Cathedral and 'Music for All'. This was, of course, news to many at the dinner, who had known that Clifford had had musical opportunities in the Middle East during the war, but not in any detail and as Clifford had kept his memories mostly to himself, it was quite a revelation for most people that night.

Another familiar voice was that of **Arthur Reckless** (the bass, who was later to become Professor of Singing at the Guildhall School of Music and Drama), also bringing back memories from Cairo days and of music making with Clifford in post-war times. Also, there was a cable sent by the Israel Philharmonic Orchestra, with greetings and appreciation. Recorded messages were sent by soloists of a recent Special Choir performance of Elgar's 'The Apostles' in the Cathedral - **Elizabeth Simon, Barbara Rowbotham, John Carol-Case** and **Roger Stalman**. They were united in sentiments that declared that "there is no more agreeable and unflappable conductor in the whole of the business".

Antony Pooley, leader of Clifford's orchestras for about five years, paid great tribute to him on a recording, when he said what a tremendous thrill it was to work with Clifford. He said that most musicians consider him a 'musician in a million'. Then followed a recording of one of the many arr. C.H. Carols.

Alistair Jones had also been busy. He had written music specially to mark the occasion, and so the evening turned out an extremely happy and memorable one, paying tribute to this worthy gentleman. Twenty-five years was a superb achievement, not just playing for services at the Cathedral, but he was a musician first and last, giving encouragement, kindness and tolerance throughout.

A further nine years passed and Clifford was once more in the limelight at a Dinner in the Cathedral School Hall given especially for him. This time, on 16th July, **1983**, it was to celebrate thirty-four years of devoted service as he retired from his office as Organist and Master of the Choristers (a 1542 title, he regularly recalled).

Clifford took everything in his stride, though he undoubtedly felt the significance of the occasion, and kept emotions fully in check as he received all ovations and showed great jollity and appreciation of all that was being done in his honour.

A very attractive Menu and Order of Proceedings had been prepared by Norman Gough, the cover of which was a photographed copy of part of Clifford's own 'Te Deum'.

Once again, Rex Hipple made careful record of all proceedings - a tape which Clifford would surely listen to again once the excitement of the occasion had died down. Bishop Oliver Tomkin was there, as was his dear friend of 'pageant' days, Freda Hulcoop.

His good friend, **John Jenkins**, was Master of Ceremonies, paying his own personal appreciation of Clifford and all that he had meant to himself and to countless choristers over the years. He said he knew that Clifford was leaving the choir in good shape and in fine spirit. There was no fizzling out of interest or carelessness of approach but, characteristically, hard, dedicated work until the end, and the Cathedral music stood as fine as it ever did.

There was a recording of the Choristers singing, in the Cathedral, Psalm 119 to a chant by Alwyn Surplice, and a recording of 'Good King Wenceslas'. **Donald Adams** sang G&S, which reminded the whole company present of Clifford's love of opera. Donald Adams had been a Bristol chorister but whenever it was mentioned Clifford was always careful to point out that it was <u>before</u> his time! **Alwyn Surplice** sent greetings and, with customary panache, sent a recording of his choristers singing a mock chant in praise of the retiring Master. He said in all sincerity "You've got one of the best there, one of the very best".

Canon Pilkington, in his speech, said that he had found Clifford a **religious** man - in the best sense; not a pious, pompous puritan humbug, but everything musical was done for the glory of God. (This was one reason why Clifford did not like applause after a concert in the Cathedral). He found him **full-blooded** - he put everything into what he did, but he was humble, straightforward and honest. He was a **traditionalist** - but open-minded to new ideas and music. He also found Clifford **sensitive** - his choice of music, the Christmas music in particular, and was especially calm when dealing with everybody's problems at concerts (even though Clifford confessed he never slept a wink after a concert, but relived the music over and over again). He was a much loved man.

The incoming Organist, **Malcolm Archer**, also sent a message, with organ music - Clifford's Rouen Processional - recorded by him in Norwich Cathedral.

After many tributes, Clifford was at last given a chance to speak for himself. First of all, he thanked Rex Hipple for all the excellent arrangements he had made for this Retirement evening. He thanked people for gifts - one being a beautiful scale model of the Eastern Lady Chapel organ, and gifts from present choristers and lay clerks. He then had opportunity to speak of his long association with the Cathedral and had been overwhelmed with events of the past week - a **Special Choir Dinner**, then a Special concert (at which Haydn's Te Deum was sung by the Cathedral Choir - magnificent!) and a wonderful floral display. He was glad to see all his present **choristers** (they must not be late for practice tomorrow) and numerous **ex-choristers** and **Assistants**.

He paid tribute to **David Isitt**, Canon Precentor, whose musical background and liturgical innovations enhanced the work of the Cathedral.

Clifford spoke with feeling about all those with whom he had worked all those years: "I have played for the daily service more or less every day for thirty-four years, and played in Bath. The greatest joy of all has been to work with the choristers, with their liveliness and their friendship. And with the lay clerks, gentlemen of the choir, for their loyalty and their sense of commitment. It has meant absolutely everything to me, and that has been marvellous. I have sometimes thought how marvellous it would have been to be organist at somewhere, shall we say, Winchester or Durham - where they get crowds of people especially in the summer, and you get an 'audience' to sing to. Perhaps that is the wrong thing to say - we have a service and we sing to the glory of God, but it is nice to have a congregation to sing to. We don't get that in Bristol, we get the smallest number of people. But you know what happens in Bristol - when visitors come in: in Winchester or Durham there's nothing else, really, to see but the Cathedral. Here in Bristol they go to the Suspension Bridge, and they go to the Zoo; they go to see King Street and to see the Theatre; they go to a certain Parish Church not far from here (meaning St. Mary Redcliffe) and then, if there's time, they come and see the Cathedral. Many people have lived in Bristol all their life and have never been to the Cathedral. I've been lucky in that I've had three choral societies where we get all the audience and the applause, so I've really had the best of both worlds".

With all good humour Clifford said he had heard that someone had said, about the music of the new Prayer Book: "Harker is being difficult". Tongue-in-cheek, he responded to this: "I was so surprised because **everybody** knows I'm never difficult." (Tumultuous applause and tremendous, typical, laugh from the man himself).

It was a memorable event for everyone present.

People best qualified to pay tribute to Clifford's work at the Cathedral are those with whom he worked. **Canon J.M. Free**, who became Precentor about eighteen months before Clifford's retirement, made the following observations which easily underline the feelings of many, not least those people whose words and memories are interwoven in this chapter:

'I remember him with affection. It was the quality of his life and the spirit with which he carried out his work which I remember best. He was unfailing in his courtesy to all, young and old, and his gentle discipline of choristers meant that there will be many who looked up to him then, and who will remember him now with great respect and thankfulness. He had care for every aspect of work in the Cathedral, not least as a Trustee of the Choral Foundation which raised money to continue the choral tradition. When he retired he made no attempt to influence his successor, in spite of his long service to the Cathedral, and he quietly left. His own spiritual life was one of high integrity, and it would hardly be exaggerated to speak of his holiness.'

Stephen Foulkes remembers: "Came the very sad day when Clifford conducted his last Evensong with the Cathedral Choir. It was a very emotional experience! The music included the Psalms set to Clifford's chants, the canticles Murrill in E, and the anthem was Brahms' 'How lovely are Thy dwellings' from the German Requiem - the work which was the first Clifford had conducted with the Special Choir when he formed it in 1953. Everybody stayed in their place while he played his last voluntary - Widor's Toccata - and then he processed out with the choir. After a vestry prayer he came round to shake everybody's hand, and his eyes were wet with tears. It must have been very difficult for him."

Another great 'chapter' completed!

CHAPTER 4
CHOIRS, ORCHESTRAS, SOLOISTS
'Our souls with high music ringing'

Rugby

Post-war music making by the nation as a whole was a refreshing and positive stimulus and Clifford's influence in the Warwickshire town of Rugby was soon felt. His idea of forming a choral society was a welcome and popular strategy, and soon the new choir began to give performances from the great musical cornucopia: without any doubt Messiah would come high on the list of regular works, with Brahms' 'Requiem' and Dvorak 'Stabat Mater' in the forefront of the choir's repertoire.

Never doing anything by halves, Clifford ensured high quality performances by engaging well-known soloists, names which included his good friend **Arthur Reckless**, (who was once again picking up the threads of civilian life), and **Isobel Baillie**.

Clifford was the mainstay of the structure, whilst eminent organists were invited to accompany the performances, together with a small orchestra in which his friend **John Bennett** played viola.

Notable accompanists gave strong support on the organ - **Dr. George Cunningham**, sometime organist at Alexandra Palace and Birmingham Town Hall. He was also conductor of the City of Birmingham Choir and a leading organ recitalist throughout the country in his day. **Dr. Henry Ley**, organist and Master of Music at Christ Church Cathedral, Oxford (becoming Precentor of Eton College) also played for Clifford's concerts, as did **Dr. Harold Darke**, Examiner at the Royal College of Organists and organist at St. Michael's, Cornhill, London.

Also to honour Clifford by accompanying at his concerts was **Dr. George Thalben-Ball** (knighted 1982) who, at the time, was organist and Director of Music at Temple Church, London, and Music Adviser to the BBC Religious Broadcasting Department. Dr. Thalben-Ball was prominent on the committee which produced the BBC Hymn Book, The Broadcast Psalter, and New Every Morning. He gave organ recitals until very late in life.

Clifford's influence in Rugby remained for a long time after he had moved to Bristol, and his choral society flourished for many years.

Bristol

On arriving at Bristol, it was quite evident that the place was teeming with musical activity, and musical societies of all types and sizes abounded, many having existed for a considerable time.

Nor was religious music to be found only in the Cathedral. Every City church had its own choir, providing a good standard of musical enrichment to services - even the non-conformist houses of prayer resounded on Sundays in resplendent strains of praise to The Almighty, in choirs of worthy proportions, often to the creditable accompaniment of sizeable orchestras in addition to their organs. Clifford viewed all this musical talent with interest, for it was reminiscent of his north-country experiences.

This was the beginning of his fifty years' association with Bristol, becoming one of the West's finest conductors. With his choirs he gave numerous performances of the great choral works, enjoying an easy rapport with many of the country's leading soloists of the day. His choirs, orchestras and, indeed, his soloists, adored him for the warmth he generated among them as a 'family' of musicians, and for his infectious enthusiasm and boundless energy in communicating a love of what he regarded a supreme form of music-making.

His personality exploded ebulliently when confronted by the massed forces of choir and orchestra; he was a wonderful conductor with great technical command, flair, and enthusiasm, through which the music flowed effortlessly. Whatever the size of his choir, he was at home with them all - the smaller ensemble work of his Cathedral choir, a choir of thirty-six singing 'Messiah' (which he conducted for Robin Walker at Glastonbury), to the splendid sonorities that filled the Cathedral, Colston Hall and Bath Abbey - each one a memorable performance.

Clifford had the same consideration for all his choirs. Every year he went personally to London, to the agents Ibbs and Tillett, to book the whole season's soloists for all three societies. This, he knew, was wise practice because if ever a soloist was unable to perform it was relatively easy to obtain a replacement quickly, at a moment's notice. It rarely happened, though, that he was faced with this kind of problem, but there was the guarantee of obtaining the services of a singer of similar standing.

Ibbs and Tillett's agency necessitated a day's journey, but Clifford willingly made the train journey as he knew he would receive wise guidance from a lady employee who intuitively knew his needs and on whom he could rely to get the best people. She knew personally all the soloists and all their repertoire, and was a great help when Clifford wanted to engage soloists for his programmes. He knew what he needed - people with voices that could fill the Colston Hall, or good operatic singers when he was performing dramatic works. He found he never got quite the same personal, satisfactory, service after the lady retired, finding that he had to deal with several different representatives at the agency.

Once the engagement contract was fixed, Clifford sent soloists full details of date, place, rehearsal times, and any notes about the works being performed with any deviation from the full score. At the rehearsal someone (often the Chairman) was posted to look out for soloists arriving. Clifford Harker would welcome them individually at an appropriate point in the rehearsal, introducing them to the choir and orchestra who would respond with welcoming applause.

At the end of the rehearsal soloists were regularly taken to tea and given facilities for rest and changing for the performance. Committee members would offer this hospitality or any member would be glad to entertain soloists in this way. **Alan McCulloch**, one time Chairman of the Bristol Choral Society offered generous hospitality on many occasions, once entertaining **Malcolm Williamson**, (Master of the Queen's Musick) for a whole weekend when the choir was performing his newly completed 'Mass of Christ the King', with its pre-concert talk.

On the evening of the concert again soloists would be duly looked after and taken to the Artistes' Room, shared by Clifford Harker and orchestra leader, and served with light refreshments during the interval. There were many behind-the -scenes matters to be arranged whenever there was a concert, and soloists greatly appreciated the kind gesture, especially if they were in unfamiliar surroundings.

Many soloists commented upon Clifford's warm welcome and utmost decorum. He earned the highest regard of many visiting musicians, most of whom were nationally, often internationally, renowned and when Clifford's retirement eventually happened tributes to his admirable musicianship were paid to him by many artistes. Conversely, though, if any soloist withdrew from a contract, or showed unprofessional behaviour, they were never invited again by him (illness excepted, naturally). On the whole, soloists were well chosen and were one hundred per cent reliable.

Clifford would never consider a performance well and truly finished until he had written many personal letters of thanks afterwards - to principal soloists, key orchestral players, and did not forget to thank minor soloists who may have been a local singer brought in for a small part, or a choir member whose part was to sing only a few bars - all were given the same 'Clifford' treatment of genuine, courteous, appreciation and gratitude for their services.

When it did come to retirement, notable solo singers who had had the joy of working with Clifford were generous with their own appreciative comments:

The soprano, **Penelope Price-Jones** regretted his going and jokingly said she would miss particularly singing the first few bars of 'Rejoice greatly' at the rehearsal, and that Clifford was possibly the fastest rehearsal-maker in the business of Messiah - but added that the performances never suffered.

Helen Attfield (alto) said she was glad of opportunities to sing those marvellous works with Clifford, particularly Elgar's 'Gerontius', with which he had special affinity. She had never been as happy singing the Angel with any other conductor.

David Johnston (tenor), one of the finest ever exponents of the tenor role of Gerontius, exclaimed "Heavens! Where would Bristol music have been these thirty-odd years without Clifford's inspiring influence and leadership?" He said that like so many professional colleagues, he had a host of reasons to be eternally grateful to Clifford over the years - for the warmth of his friendship and the enormous amount learned under his guidance. If one composer stood out as one whose music Clifford's expertise had most richly served, it would have to be Elgar - The Apostles, The Kingdom and, of course, 'The Dream'. He confided that once Clifford had paid him an enormous compliment. Clifford told him "It was so easy, it was as if we'd always performed that work together." (This was probably Gerontius.) In return, David said he was prepared to say that without Clifford that performance would have been impossible.

David Johnston recalled with affection how, at exactly the appointed time, Clifford would get on the rostrum and, with courtesy, would introduce the soloists to the choir and orchestra, and then that 'stick' would come down . . . . and from the first note the score would unfold almost as if by magic, and he would spend the next couple of hours or so drawing out of everyone the sorts of sounds that many didn't think they were capable of.

Roger Stalman declared there was no more agreeable and unflappable conductor in the whole of the business.

Another popular visiting soloist to Bristol was **Raimond Herincx**. He once told David Jewell that, when singing the part of the Dutchman in a concert version of Wagner's 'The Flying Dutchman', in the Colston Hall, a three-hour rehearsal left forty-five minutes' singing unrehearsed. He said that Clifford was the only conductor in the country he would do that with.

Brian Rayner-Cook was also a welcome soloist with all three societies, who said he was always glad to be singing for Clifford. He stated to David Jewell that he never failed to learn from Clifford. In a conversation with David once he told him that it was common knowledge that no conductor in the country obeyed Elgar's instructions. In the part of the Angel of the Agony (Gerontius) the crotchet is marked 48. "Nobody takes it at 48," he said, "and I always insist that they do." He was once asked "Are you going to insist that Clifford Harker does that?" He replied "Oh, no, I shalln't do it with Clifford. He can take it at what speed he likes, because Clifford is an Elgarian."

When he came to the Cathedral in 1976 for a performance of The Kingdom, Brian Rayner-Cook experienced a charming incident. He had noticed a lady sitting in the Nave during the rehearsal and during a short break she spoke to Clifford. When the rehearsal ended, Clifford said to everyone "Ladies and gentlemen, I have to tell you the rehearsal was marvellous. That was Elgar's daughter, Mrs. Elgar-Blake. She said she was so delighted with the way in which we are going to perform tonight."

Carice Elgar-Blake lived in Westbury on Trym, Bristol, for a number of years and so it was not surprising that she expressed a keen interest and encouragement whenever her father's music was being performed. It was in February, 1968, that she wrote the following letter to Clifford:

Dear Mr. Harker,
> Please forgive this intrusion, but I do want to say how pleased I am to see you have included my father's Sursum Corda in your very interesting programme on March 3rd. My friend .... (a cellist by the way) much hopes to come.

> I have so much wanted to tell you how enormously impressed I was with your performance of The Kingdom - you had every shade and nuance of expression - your reading was perfect - and the soloists and orchestra responded marvellously - I never hope to hear a better performance.
>
> Yours sincerely,
> C. Elgar Blake (Mrs.)

References to Elgar's music was endorsement that many people learned to love this composer's works through Clifford. He excelled in Elgar and, because of his own insight, would always take time to talk about a particular work once rehearsals had started in order to give singers a greater understanding and appreciation of the composition **as a whole**, and not just as a performance. For instance, he would discuss Elgar's choice of text, particularly for The Apostles and The Kingdom and delighted in indicating in these works (as well as in The Music Makers) how Elgar had 'borrowed' his own phrases from works such as Enigma and the Symphonies. When preparing 'Gerontius' he indicated the various 'themes' as the Overture revealed the glorious melodies in the work. This kind of introduction helped to give more meaningful insight into both words and music.

The Special Choir held particularly pleasant memories of Gerontius when **Janet Baker** (before she had won deserved fame) sang the part of the Angel, and what conductor, except perhaps Boult, could conjure sounds like Clifford's Elgar performances from enthusiastic amateurs?

Because of his great love of Elgar's music, when performing his works Clifford particularly wanted everything to go well. **Canon David Isitt** remembered a significant incident which happened shortly before the Special Choir was due to perform 'Gerontius' (a special favourite of Clifford's) in 1983. Clifford was, of course, a consummate bachelor and, as such, found occasional pitfalls which he had to overcome. Clifford advanced David one day in the Cathedral cloister, waving a letter he had just received, with a look of abject horror on his face. "It's from the Angel," he said, "she says she's pregnant! What am I to do?". David had much trouble persuading him that it probably would not show, and that most mezzo-sopranos looked as though they were pregnant, anyway. Just before the concert, Clifford whispered to David "I think it's going to be all right."

Clifford was not only a perfectionist in his own sphere but he had the happy knack of bringing out the best in his singers and players; indeed, he did more than that - his sensitive interpretation made singers (and instrumentalists) bring out the best in themselves. He had the artistry to create a devotional atmosphere when performing a sacred work in the Colston Hall (Handel's Messiah being the supreme example). This was never just first class performance but a sincere and relevant offering of words and music.

Michael Doswell's remarks in relation to Clifford's quite magical interpretations echo the opinion of many people. He said "He did an electrifying Verdi Requiem, and as an interpreter of Elgar he had few equals. I can still hear the note of censure in his voice when I told him that 'The Dream of Gerontius' (a work very close to his heart) was, for me, too Catholic. I might as well have hurled a brick through the Cathedral's stained glass windows! Of all the choral masterpieces, the one that stays most vividly in the memory is Bach's St. Matthew Passion, particularly the passage set to the words 'Truly, this was the Son of God', which had a special meaning for him. During those few bars his eyes would glaze over, and his singers would experience, as if through some invisible current, the deep intensity of that moment.

"As an aspiring musician I picked up much useful knowledge - watching, listening and, importantly, observing, how to handle people, for which he had an enviable gift. I only ever saw him extremely irritated once, when the Dean famously described a performance of Vaughan Williams' 'Dona Nobis Pacem' (of all pieces!) as "rather jolly".

"He said to me "I try to give emotional performances, musicians seem to appreciate it." Indeed, they do, and what I learned from Clifford when I formed an orchestra in the North-east was how to convey music, as opposed to merely beating time.

"During the course of a very instructive conducting lesson he (Clifford) said to me "Remember, controlling your players is concerned with being clear with the point of the stick. It is about anticipating what you want to happen, what you say with your eyes, and economy of gesture." His own conducting, at least in those early days, seemed to me to be a bit on the expansive side, and a little at odds with the advice he gave but, of course, he was generous in everything he did.

"Clifford once said to me "Always encourage a choir, and if you have to criticise, do it kindly." He always followed his own advice, telling a section of the Special Choir, for example, that their singing was very good in some passage or other, but with more than a hint of I-didn't-really-think-so in his voice. More typically, he would deliver a characteristic witticism which generally led to an improvement when the laughter had died down."

Clifford made available a range of choral works, well known and unfamiliar, not only to his choirs and orchestras but to a public willing to be educated at his hands. Having three large choral societies meant that each week more than six hundred singers rehearsed under his baton in addition to the Cathedral Choir, and it is quite true to say that he generated tremendous loyalty, giving to people considerable pleasure and satisfaction which comes from learning and performing choral music. He was kind-hearted, amicable and entertaining as a conductor, drawing the best from his choirs by encouragement and persuasion.

He planned and made preparation for his concerts most carefully, even teaching himself German so that he could get to grips with the Bach Passions. Preparation was always done well before rehearsals started, even when they were not new to him; most of his summer holiday was spent working on scores. Particular study was necessary when preparing difficult works like Malcolm Williamson's 'Mass of Christ the King' - which had to be learned from poorly duplicated manuscript copy and very difficult to read - or Raymond Warren's 'Continuing Cities'. Clifford had a great ability to rehearse singers without patronising them but knowing ultimately how to get them round the notes. He saw the human potential of even the weakest singer and the way in which they were contributing of themselves - how important it was for their sense of self-worth. He knew how satisfying it was for people when tackling difficult music, to overcome problems and to have made a creditable performance.

Clifford made prudent selection of works to be performed and, though he had his own favourites, it was not just a matter of choosing a mixture of old favourites and new works; there were other important factors to be considered when making a choice. One vital aspect was orchestration. Size of orchestra needed to be right for the whole programme in any one concert, thus making full use of orchestral resources. The orchestra should also balance choir numbers, and although concerts were principally choral, occasionally an orchestral item, often an overture, was added to balance the programme and give the audience 'value for money'. Concert versions of operas were rarely given, however enjoyable, because there was never enough for the chorus to rehearse. At the other end of the scale, a difficult work like Florent Schmitt Psalm 47 proved troublesome to learn and needed extra rehearsal time; even so, it was not good enough for Clifford's satisfaction by the time the Bristol Choral Society concert for which it was scheduled and so a substitute item became necessary, giving more time for the work to be prepared satisfactorily for the next concert. This unfortunate occurrence happened only once in the whole of Clifford's period with BCS; normally his choir was thoroughly prepared in time for the performance date.

Rehearsals were, for many people, the most important night of the week, as Clifford guided singers through in his own inimitable way. It seemed to many of them a tremendous privilege to be able to experience those great works in such a place and under such a great conductor, a feeling which never left many of his singers.

Clifford's conducting style was undoubtedly influenced by Sir Malcolm Sargent, though without too much flamboyance. He could use excited gestures during some choruses like The Hallelujah, especially the King of Kings entries towards the end. He had his own favourite moments - one of them in Messiah, when the music changes at the end of the Overture to the first major chord of 'Comfort ye'. When his choirs reached the final 'Amen' they felt they had witnessed a profound affirmation of faith as well as a musical *tour de force*. Much as he loved 'The Dream', he was much affected by the phrase in Elgar's The Apostles 'And the Lord turned, and looked upon Peter', and the soul-piercing phrase in Bach's St. Matthew Passion 'Truly, this was the Son of God'; and it was not difficult to understand why he felt they were for him the most perfect examples of musical portrayal ever written.

There were always times of light relief, and in a lifetime consumed by music, this was often to be found in the works of Gilbert and Sullivan. Clifford would revel in concert performances of these operettas with stars of the D'Oyley Carte, amongst whom were **Donald Adams** (a former Bristol Chorister), **Thomas Round** and **John Reid**. He used to love telling his students how, when himself a student, he was surprised to see **Constant Lambert** (one of his tutors at RCM) sitting at a table in a restaurant, with a score propped up in front of him, conducting with a sauce bottle, looking up and saying "Hello, Harker, just look what this fellow does here!" and going on conducting.

Bristol Madrigal Society (1949 - 1955)

To return to Clifford's arrival in Bristol in 1949, he very quickly found himself following Alwyn Surplice, not only at the Cathedral, but in the post of Musical Director of the Bristol Madrigal Society, practically the oldest musical society in Britain. This he was keen to do, and he remained with them until 1955.

Madrigal singing had been popular in the heart of Bristol for over a century. January, 1837, had been the date when 'some gentlemen who were very desirous to promote Madrigal singing in this City, met at Mr. Austin Phillips's to consider of the practicability of forming a Society for that purpose'. Already there were various glee clubs in existence in Bristol, but some members found the beauty and superiority of madrigals attractive and from that date the Society enjoyed great success, meeting fortnightly at the Montague Inn in Kingsdown (destroyed by bombs in 1940) until 1922. From then on meetings were held at the Music Club in Clifton. For many years it was a totally male assemblage, comprising seven choristers from the Cathedral who sang the treble parts, while the six male altos, eight tenors and seven basses included four Cathedral lay clerks. This original number included for a time Robert Lucas Pearsall (born in 1795) a talented amateur string player and singer, whose 'madrigals' were eventually allowed to be sung alongside the true madrigals of the Golden Age. They sat at tables in circular fashion, with 'a weak singer sitting between two strong ones'. Their first programmes consisted of early madrigals by Bennet, Gibbons, Morley, Weelkes, and other early composers, and copies used were single-voice parts. By the end of the first year they had accumulated a collection of seventy-six works.

From the first, the annual Ladies' Nights were popular becoming fashionable social functions, and at one time milliners showed in their windows costumes that had been ordered for the coming Madrigal Concert.

Most Ladies' Nights were held in the Victoria Rooms, the principal venue for eighty-two years. These occasions remained popular for many years at which the custom was to sing the **National Anthem** to a setting by William Worsley (1774-1858) at the commencement, and '**The Waits**' by Jeremiah Savile (17th century) at the close. The singing of 'The Waits' to conclude meetings had been adopted from the beginning, and continues to this day.

This short piece is interesting in that originally it was sung only to 'Fa la la' in harmony, but words were set later, and various renderings may be given but, to be entirely accurate, the piece should be sung four times: first - forte, secondly - piano, thirdly - pianissimo, fourthly - fortissimo. This jolly custom is loved by all Bristol Madrigalians:

>Let us all sing, merrily sing,
>Let us all sing, merrily sing,
>Till echo around us, responsive shall sing.
>Fa la la.

(Perhaps there was no need for Clifford to conduct that one!)

Numbers gradually increased and eventually fixed at sixty. In 1885, the members travelled to London to give a performance in the Royal Albert Hall at the Council of International Inventions Exhibition, and they gave a short programme in 1908 before their majesties King Edward VII and Queen Alexandra aboard the Royal Yacht in Avonmouth Dock.

From 1919 the Society began to include madrigals by later composers, and anthems. In addition to the early madrigals newly added works were by Pearsall, Parry, Stanford, Walford-Davies and Napier-Miles. A number of pieces were written expressly for the Madrigal Society. From 1923, instrumental accompaniment was included in their recital programmes. Dr. Hubert Hunt (Organist at the Cathedral) was Musical Director from 1915 to 1945, and Alwyn Surplice held that post until 1946 until he left for Winchester in 1949. The baton then passed to Clifford Harker until 1955.

In early post-war years numbers totalled 51, comprising 19 sopranos, 10 altos, 11 tenors and 11 basses.

It was Alwyn Surplice who took the first steps to re-form the Society after a lapse during the war years (1939-45). Boy trebles were not available, mainly due to changes in school routine, and so membership was reconstituted to include ladies, who would sing the upper parts. The advent of ladies to the Society was **quite** a landmark as one of the rules from the founding had been that 'No lady be admitted to the room while meetings were progressing.' A male consort had been considered 'correct' for early madrigals, but when the Society began to introduce motets and larger choral works, women's voices proved fully justified. Ladies began to hold office, also, and Miss Enid Hunt, daughter of Dr. Hubert Hunt, became (at various times) Assistant Secretary, Hon. Librarian and Vice-President.

Clifford Harker was delighted with his new choir and arranged his first public programme in March, 1950, to be held in Bristol Cathedral. It included two motets by Bach and chorales related to Bach Preludes played on the organ - by Clifford Harker. This was part of the Bristol Bach Festival to mark the 200th Anniversary of the composer's death.

Under their new Musical Director, the Madrigal Society gave concerts usually in a hall - the Victoria Rooms mostly - but, also, programmes were given in the Galleries of the Royal West of England Academy, in the Museum Lecture Theatre and Bristol University, as well as in the Cathedral. The Society participated regularly in the musical life of Bristol. Performances under Clifford were often given with a small orchestra, which was later to form the nucleus of the Special Choir Orchestra. Several concerts were performed with the BBC West of England Singers before Clifford formed his Cathedral Special Choir in 1953.

Clifford's period with the Madrigal Society was to last for six years and in 1955 he was obliged to resign due to pressure of work elsewhere. Since its foundation, four out of five Musical Directors had been the current organist of the Cathedral. After Clifford, the tradition was broken by the appointment of Mr. Herbert Byard, a writer and lecturer at Bristol University.

Later recitals by the Society, particularly those in the Cathedral, included larger choral works which included Byrd motets and Masses by Palestrina, and early music being performed for the first time in Bristol. However, the choir still retained the full repertory of English and Italian madrigals, and members still derived the aesthetic pleasure of a small choir singing some of the most beautiful music ever written.

Much later than Clifford's period with the Madrigal Society (1988), in order to reflect the inclusion of a more extensive repertoire, the choir was renamed '**Bristol Chamber Choir (under the auspices of Bristol Madrigal Society)**' and '**The Waits**' is still sung to this day.

Bristolians had enjoyed hearing choral music on a grand scale for more than sixty years and music-making groups abounded. In addition to the more intimate numbers of the Madrigal Society, the **Royal Orpheus Glee Society**, and a number of local glee and catch clubs, **Bristol Philharmonic Society** was a large and popular organisation. There was also the **Bristol Triennial Music Festival**, calling for massed voices which sang under its renowned conductor, **Sir Charles Hallé**. This Festival choir, in 1912, then under **George Riseley**, gave the first concert rendering in English of Wagner's 'Der Ring des Nibelungen'.

George Riseley was much involved in Bristol music and from 1876 to 1899 was Organist and Master of the Choristers at the Cathedral. He gathered together nearby choirs to form a **Festival Choir** of 400 voices, which gave four performances over two days (programmes including Mendelssohn's Elijah) as part of the celebrations for **Queen Victoria's Golden Jubilee** in 1887. In 1888, this same choir, plus a further 300 voices, gave four concerts to mark the completion of the Cathedral's western towers. On these occasions music performed included Israel in Egypt (Handel), Dettingen Te Deum (Handel) and Hymn of Praise (Mendelssohn). Even earlier than 1888, George Riseley led a small group known as the **Cathedral Amateur Choral Society**, giving regular musical evenings. Bristol Choral Society 'grew' from these occasions. George Riseley also trained an orchestra of local players and gave a series of **Monday 'Pops'** concerts in the Colston Hall as well as conducting the **Bristol Society of Instrumentalists** - the largest amateur orchestra in the country. He was another giant in Bristol musical circles!

Moving into the twentieth century, another notable musician, **Arnold Barter**, was conductor of the Bristol Philharmonic Society for fifty years. This large society rehearsed in the Museum Lecture Theatre, giving concerts in the Colston Hall, but suffered many problems and, after struggling through the Second World War finally disbanded, leaving a large void in choral circles. Clifford Harker was approached but, mainly through difficulties of funding, the situation had deteriorated too much to resurrect.

Bristol Cathedral Special Choir (1954-83)

Events in Bristol requiring celebratory music were beginning to occur following a gradual return to normality after the effects of the war. In **1950** there was a festival in Bristol to mark the bi-Centenary of Bach's death and different organisations performed on different nights; then, in 1951 the whole nation celebrated with a Festival of Britain - a wonderful morale-booster. During these years Clifford arranged various choral events, augmenting local choirs, and during 1953, the year of the Coronation of Her Majesty Queen Elizabeth II, opportunities for very special choral events abounded, bringing people together to sing in large numbers again.

It was following the great success of these occasions that Clifford had the idea of continuing with a choral society of his own, both rehearsing and giving concerts in the Cathedral. So he set about forming such a choir, to be named the Bristol Cathedral Special Choir.

Notices were put out in the local Press, which proved most productive; the Cathedral community made it known; Clifford told his choristers to ask their parents, aunts and uncles; in fact, much was done to encourage enough people to meet to form the new choir.

A small committee met with Clifford in July of 1953, which included Mr. Graham Hooper (Organist of the Lord Mayor's Chapel), who was to be accompanist. This committee discussed details of the formation of the choir, setting up a policy, and appointing a secretary and treasurer, with the Dean as President.

The method of selecting singers for the choir was by private audition and, for a time, Clifford was busy seeing applicants. People found him amenable and fair, many remembering how he instilled confidence, even during an audition. In his music room in the cloisters he first asked applicants to sing a few voice exercises, followed by a sight reading test. This was a portion of Brahms' Requiem (How lovely are Thy dwellings fair) which was to be sung at the inaugural concert.

Many members of the former Bristol Philharmonic Society joined, together with a substantial number already belonging to other choirs in the area. More than a few were members of both Bristol Choral Society and the Special Choir during the whole period of Clifford's conductorship, getting a double helping of singing every week under the Harker baton.

By the time rehearsals commenced in October, 1953, the new choir numbered 203, which was a large enough body for Cathedral performances, and a further 25 names were kept on the waiting list. Members paid an annual subscription of half a guinea (10s.6p.) for the season October to March, and were asked to provide their own music. Rehearsals were held at the Cathedral on Mondays, from 7.30 to 9.0 p.m.

From the start, singers caught the enthusiasm that welled up from within this man, and gained confidence to extend their own capabilities. He would ask them to "let the heavens open" in the 'everlasting joy' passages of the Brahms, causing even the second sopranos to soar towards a top B flat. This particular artistic encouragement brought about a memorable moment when the work was performed. The Press made the following comment: 'So the most memorable moment came, as it always should, after the stern tumult and bitter anxiety of the funeral march had died down, and in the 'everlasting joy' there was a serene rejoicing, a feeling of aspiration as truly spiritual and joyous as anything ever sung in Bristol'. The Press remarks also stated: 'The choristers made a lovely thing of the fifth movement. The Requiem was sung with deep devotion and inspiration, with infinite grandeur and profound understanding. Bristol is indeed fortunate in having so enterprising an artiste and musician as Mr. Clifford Harker, who does not spare himself in making possible such an occasion as last evening's performance'.

Clifford started as he meant to go on. To him, all music-making was a form of Christian worship, and he would always retire in private prayer with the Dean a few minutes before every concert in the Cathedral.

Further Press comment was positive and encouraging: 'Despite the absence this season of the Philharmonic Society, choral music flourished and Mr. Clifford Harker's Cathedral Special Choir got away to an excellent start with a fine performance of Brahms' German Requiem, which will long be remembered by those who heard it.'

The programme had been announced by the Press beforehand, being described as 'a Requiem for all creeds' - the setting, not of the normal liturgical texts, but words taken from the German Bible by Brahms himself. It proved a good choice for première of this new venture as it was a work with which Clifford was already familiar, having performed it in Cairo in 1944 and in Rugby. One great disappointment in the event, for Clifford, was the absence through illness of his good friend Arthur Reckless, who was to have sung the baritone solos. Instead, Frederick Harvey (who became a frequent soloist during the next few years) sang the baritone parts, whilst the Soprano solo was sung by the Cathedral choristers. The eminent Bristol violinist, **Edwin Brown**, was leader of the augmented orchestra, and the programme for the evening made interesting reading, costing two shillings, whilst admission to the concert was free!

Having taken off with such tremendous success, Clifford was much delighted and encouraged to plan ahead, keeping his feet firmly on the ground by assuring members at the Annual General Meeting in May, 1954 (first stating with typical humour that his report would be in two movements, neither of which would be slow) that he wished to attain the highest standard of performance stressing that the choir must pay its way. He commented also that he had experienced much enthusiasm, which was particularly obvious by extremely good attendances during the severe winter. He was able to express much confidence in his new choir and was already making plans far into the future. ....at the time, he could not possibly realise that it would be one of his most enjoyable activities for the next thirty years.

So started the long association with the Special Choir which, to many members, became the most important part of their life. Clifford was an inspiration to the whole choir and their loyalty was unquestionable. Special Choir concerts were 'magical' - a unique experience for many choir members, and this was Clifford's **own** choir; he was engaged by a committee for his other choirs, but this one existed expressly for him to fulfil his own desire to provide people with lovely music which was entirely his own choice.

General procedure for concerts was quickly established, and Clifford did much in the background. On the morning of a concert he arrived early at the Cathedral, setting out chairs and putting reserved (named) tickets on chairs. He prepared all the choir seating tickets also, and would meticulously put out numbers for choir seating on the chairs. This ensured that the voices were positioned exactly as he required. There was no 'Green Room' in the Cathedral for choir, and members just quietly found their seats and waited for the performance to begin. When there was no interval it was the same procedure in reverse at the end of the concert.

In the very early performances there was no concert dress and, as concerts always came during the winter months (and before days of central heating) most ladies wore winter coats, many also wearing their best hat - but there was always a request that they did not put on anything too large or sensational! When the Cathedral heating arrangements improved, the standard concert dress became white blouse and long black skirt, with the gentlemen wearing black tie evening dress.

Normally, as concerts were held on Friday evenings, the rehearsal with the orchestra was in the afternoon, when most of the choir could not be there. Remarkably, though, there were few disasters and most blemishes were more evident to the performers than to the audience.

Gerry Nichols, an ex-chorister, sang in the Special Choir under Clifford for many years. He commented "I have never sung under a conductor with so clear a beat and a way of showing you with his body what he wanted, and how to get it. When there was a major entry, if you watched

25. Bristol Cathedral Special Choir rehearsal in the Colston Hall, Bristol, with the Bournemouth Symphony Orchestra, November, 1957.

Clifford, you came in at the right time and in the right way. I have also heard singers and players say that he could reproduce in the concert exactly the same tempi agreed at rehearsal. This is a remarkable achievement, considering the amount of adrenaline that a concert can cause to flow. It is also remarkable that concerts were performed with a choir and orchestra playing together for the first time."

Gerry also remembered Clifford quoting the skill of Malcolm Sargent when the choir was once having difficulty with the rhythm of a certain piece. Clifford said he had seen Sargent stand and tap his head with his right hand in 2/4 time, tap his stomach with his left hand in ¾ time, and tap his foot in 5/4!

Another chorister, **Lionel Pike**, told how he experienced tremendous excitement when he sang under Clifford's baton in Elgar's The Kingdom, and finding out how Elgar had scored the plainsong 'O sacrum convivium'. Like so many, he greatly valued having been brought up with the St. Matthew Passion, the B minor Mass, and Gerontius.

Clifford remarked at one committee meeting that success was not measured by concerts but by the weekly rehearsals. The strength of the Choir depended upon its enthusiasm and he always looked forward to, and enjoyed, Monday evenings.

It became a regular practice to give two concerts annually from the sacred repertoire (The Carol Concerts will be discussed later) and from 1953 until his retirement in 1983 his choir had the thrill of performing works of the great masters - these are listed in detail in Appendix II.

Soloists were top-ranking, and gave superb interpretations of the works being performed, but space does not allow for a comprehensive list of solo singers. Exceptionally fine artistes were **Jennifer Vyvyan** (soprano) and **Pamela Bowden** (alto) in Elgar's The Kingdom; **Wilfred Brown** (tenor), **Heather Harper** (soprano) and **Janet Baker** (mezzo) who, with **Thomas Round** and **John Carol-Case** gave memorable performances in the Bach Passions and Verdi Requiem, with **David Johnston** and **Brian Rayner-Cook** in Gerontius. Rarely did any soloist fall below Clifford's own high standards, both by interpretation and professionalism.

Clifford put on Handel's Messiah with the Special Choir only once. It was an amicable arrangement with the Bristol Choral Society that they should not interrupt the age-old custom of performing this work in the Colston Hall each year. However, in 1963, the Special Choir gave a first-class performance in the Cathedral, which was considered an appropriate work to offer for the Cathedral Restoration Appeal as well as the tenth anniversary concert of the Choir. However, the Hallelujah Chorus was a regular item in carol concert programmes.

One major concern that Clifford had was to ensure that as many people as possible, from all walks of life, should be able to enjoy the good music of the Cathedral and for this reason all early concerts were entirely free. Programmes cost two shillings for the first concert, two shillings and six pence for the next concert and, by 1960, a programme was still sold at 'two and six' - but - if you bought it in advance through a member or at the Cathedral, it entitled you to a seat in the centre of the Nave, provided you were in place by 7.15 p.m. In 1961, you could become a Subscriber for the two main concerts of the following season for three shillings and six pence, and this would reserve for you one of the best seats in the centre of the Nave, and your programme would also be posted to you beforehand. There was always a musical bonus through being early as there was organ music played by the Assistant Organist between 6.45 and 7.15 p.m. What value for money - even in those days!

Thus continued a long period of success, which Clifford began and built up, the Choir giving concerts that were a pleasure to hundreds of people. The Choir packed the Cathedral as nothing else did.

Graham Hooper continued to enjoy accompanying the Choir until ill health compelled him to retire, and Lionel Pike filled in for a time. **Michael Dyer** was appointed Accompanist in 1960, followed by **Robin Walker** in 1962, and **John Jenkins** in 1971. **Stephen Taylor** helped for a while, and **Alistair Jones**, **Martin Schellenberg** and **Matthew Bale** all became official choir accompanists in succession.

Carol Concerts

Charting the history of the Special Choir, however briefly, would be setting down only half the story without mention of the annual Carol Concerts. They became a tradition in their own right during Clifford's period and still continue to this day as a regular event before Christmas.

From the beginning of the Choir Clifford held a weekday evening concert of Carols and Christmas music, the first taking place on 21st December, 1954. There was a great thirst for good pre-Christmas music in Bristol. Many organisations held their own concerts - the Colston Hall was always packed for Messiah - and the Special Choir's offering was immediately thrilling, becoming a most sought-after event. Programmes were always sold out weeks in advance and, as no seats were reserved, queues would start to form outside the Cathedral during the afternoon with people wanting to obtain good seats. Even so, crowds without programmes turned up in the hope that there would be a vacant seat, and many had to be turned away. This was the situation for years and years even when, in 1963, the same programme was repeated on a second evening becoming the regular pattern for future years. There was never enough room for all who wanted to hear the wonderful music.

What was it that made these events so popular? One does not really need to answer that question, as not only was the Cathedral an ideal situation where the story of Christ's birth should be unfolded as Christmastime came round once more, but Clifford's skill in choosing worthy and fitting music, using his Special Choir, Cathedral Choir, organ, and a worthy orchestra, caused the atmosphere to become quite enchanting for such a rendering. The oft-heard remark "The Special Choir Concert always starts my Christmas" was sincerely meant, and the atmosphere at such times could only be described as a tremendous resounding of 'the glory of the Lord' - and Clifford carried it off each year with the same equanimity.

He had an enormous ability to choose suitable pieces, everything was in keeping with the mood of the event. From the Processional Hymn in which the congregation could join (as well as other congregational hymns), the variation in texture formed by the massed voices, (sometimes unaccompanied), the orchestral and organ accompaniment and interludes - everything created unforgettable moments.

Notwithstanding the delightful choice of carols, Clifford went even further by making his own carol arrangements. In all, twenty-seven lovely carols were given new and exciting harmonies, pieces were 'expanded' by wonderful orchestral arrangements and, altogether, his artistry with carols was beyond compare. To mention here just one example would ideally be, surely, 'Good King Wenceslas', which was orchestrated to such a degree as almost to lift off the roof from the Cathedral itself. These outstanding carol arrangements are detailed in Chapter 6.

In days when a number of eminent composers were producing books of carol arrangements, all excellent and enjoyable to perform and hear, anyone who heard Clifford's *divertissements* found them extra special and justifiably superior. His choirs, orchestras and, indeed his audiences, found them a 'real treat'.

Proceeds from carol concerts were always donated to children's charities.

Recordings

The carol concerts were invariably excellent occasions and **Rex Hipple** and others became keen to capture some of the wonderful programmes on disc. Therefore, in 1975 music from some of the most recent programmes was carefully and excellently recorded. In all, due to the foresight and first-class recording skills of Rex, four fine recordings were painstakingly made, with the support of the Friends of Bristol Cathedral:

1 Christmas in Bristol Cathedral (1975)
   (includes the bells of the Cathedral).
2 Carols and Christmas Music in Bristol Cathedral
   (December, 1976)
3 Music of Bristol Cathedral For the Christian Year (1978)
4 Keyboard Instruments in Bristol (about 1980)
   music played by Clifford Harker on the organ of Bristol
   Cathedral and on the 'Sarah Green' chamber organ in
   St. Nicholas' Church Museum. Other music played by
   David Pettit on the spinet in the Red Lodge and a
   harpsichord in the Georgian House.

This was an exciting venture, particularly knowing Clifford's feelings about making recordings, but he was the first to express delight and pride in what had been achieved. Sales of the records, as they became available, were high - many people were glad to have some permanent record of carol evenings, in particular. Special Choir members, Cathedral Choir and Choristers, and many people connected with the Cathedral in some way, bought copies. The records were certainly 'Top of the Charts' for Bristolians and a good profit was made; so much so that in due course a presentation to the Cathedral was made out of the profits of a beautiful silver ciborium.

Life in the Special Choir was eventful. As early as 1956 the Choir made four broadcasts for the BBC, and in 1963 they appeared in a Songs of Praise programme, and when the Choir was about to perform the St. Matthew Passion in 1959, Clifford gave a talk on the work, with illustrations by the Choir.

In 1959, whilst rehearsing Mozart's Mass in C minor one evening, there was a thunderstorm. Lightening hit the building, causing some masonry to fall which brought a few anxious moments for the Choir. It was the second time that lightening had struck the Cathedral; the first occasion was in 1703, when the schoolboys had to spend the night in the Chapter House, singing Psalms. Rehearsals were always enjoyable and Clifford's humour, mostly of the driest kind, often showed itself. He was given a cheque to mark the 10th Anniversary of the Choir, and he completely demolished everyone by announcing that he had used it for his work and his hobby. He had actually bought a tape-recorder - one of those dreadful machines! He once remarked how he thought attendance had increased since the installation of a new heating system in the Cathedral. His words probably rang very true!

Clifford could chide, but in his gentle and good-humoured way, whenever he failed to get the required response in rehearsal, but, once, he was known to tell the basses "You sound like diseased bagpipes!" During another rehearsal he put down the baton, left the rostrum, walked over to the basses and looked back towards his place. He exclaimed "There doesn't seem to be anything between here and where I stand, and yet you still don't follow me." A small voice came from within the basses "Who are you?" Clifford walked back to his rostrum, a wry grin on his face.

When Clifford retired from the Cathedral, it also meant giving up his Special Choir. He told them it was a personal sadness and he would greatly miss them. There was great sadness, too, and more than apparent in his singers, but there was the inevitable end to all good things and, as with the Cathedral Choir, all who had passed through would remember with pleasure and gratitude the wonderful musical experiences they had shared with him over the years. He was made an Honorary Life Vice-President of the Choir before handing over the baton to his successor, **Malcolm Archer**.

Through the very good foresight of a Special Choir member, **Roger Crudge**, who was Senior Music Librarian at Bristol Central Library, much of Clifford's carol arrangements, as well as copies of his published music, was placed safely in the Central Library Reference Section. Thus it became available to any member of the public upon request.

Bristol Choral Society (1960-1989)

When the Special Choir came into existence, it ran side-by-side with Bristol's other large choir, the Bristol Choral Society, which was by then (1953) in its seventy-first season.

This Society had enjoyed great success since its formation in 1889, huge numbers wishing to sing, and in 1896 it was decided to restrict singing numbers to 1,000 voices.

Concerts were given in the Colston Hall, except during the period 1896-99, when the Hall was rebuilt. Only two concerts were put on during those years, one in Queen's Hall, London, and the other in the Prince's Theatre, Bristol. When concerts resumed in the Colston Hall there were regular concerts in November, December, January, and March, and included frequent performances of Messiah, Elijah, Gounod's Redemption, Coleridge-Taylor's Hiawatha, Haydn's Creation and Elgar's Dream of Gerontius (first performed in 1903).

In 1903, the Society put on a costumed performance of Gounod's Faust with principal parts sung by principals from the Carl Rosa Opera Company.

Press reporting was always very much extended and elaborated in those days; not to modern tastes, perhaps, but it must be realised that newspapers were read more as a leisurely pastime, when even radio was almost non-existent, and the longer the Press account, the greater importance of the occasion. The report of a concert in May, 1911 (the programme content not now known) to celebrate the Coronation of King George V, was a sensational twenty- eight inches long. The Colston Hall scene would have been most attractive, with choir ladies wearing long, white, dresses and the gentlemen in full evening dress.

Colston Hall seat prices were never cheap, but always good value for money. For instance, In 1935 ticket prices ranged between 12/- for the President's Gallery and 2s/4d. A season ticket cost between two guineas and one guinea.

There was a time, when **George Riseley** retired, that the Committee decided to merge the Choir with the Bristol Philharmonic Society but, after many problems and disagreements on legal and administrative matters, which included battles for the rehearsal venue on Tuesday evenings at the Museum Lecture Theatre, the legalities had to be undone and the two bodies continued to operate separately.

The Choir was conducted by **Herbert Brewer** for two years, during which time (January, 1928) **Edward Elgar** came to conduct his own music in a concert. The pieces were Cockaigne Overture, The Music Makers and The Black Knight. Herbert Brewer conducted his own cantata 'Sir Patrick Spens' and S.S. Wesley's 'In exitu Israel' to complete the musical feast.

There followed a few years when the Choir was trained by a Chorus Master and invited distinguished guests conducted the performance, one of whom was **Sir Thomas Beecham**.

In 1929, **Mr. Samuel Underwood**, an organist from Stroud, was appointed conductor, and he was to stay with the Society for 29 years. He became revered and much respected for his musical skills with the Choir and he guided them through many years of excellent music-making.

In order to muster more funds in 1931, the Society organised a week-long Carnival in the Zoological Gardens, which made handsome profits, and in 1933 the fine sum of £50 was obtained as a fee from the BBC for a broadcast performance of Messiah.

Between 1934 and 1938 there also existed a small group of singing members, calling themselves '**The Choir of the Bristol Choral Society**, which gave broadcast programmes of madrigals and part-songs.

In 1939 there were 243 members. A Golden Jubilee concert was given - a performance of Mendelssohn's Elijah - which was broadcast on the radio.

During the war years the Bristol Choral Society and Bristol Philharmonic Society joined forces in order to give strength and balance to both bodies. Guest conductors during those years included **Sir Adrian Boult** and **Sir Henry Wood**. **Leslie Woodgate** (BBC Chorus-master) conducted in broadcast programmes. Wartime numbers were about 180, and the two choirs resumed separate identities in 1945. In February, 1945, the last joint programme was Hiawatha and was performed in the Methodist Central Hall, Old Market, as the Colston Hall had been destroyed by a fire.

A Festival of Thanksgiving was organised on 20th April, 1946, in the Royal Albert Hall, London, to 'commemorate the devoted efforts of our amateur choral singers during the war 1939-1945'. The chorus was made up of representatives from choral societies and the Competitive Festivals of Great Britain, brought together through the National Federation of Music Societies and the Federation of Festivals. The event was organised by the Arts Council of Great Britain and the Musicians Benevolent Fund. Many Bristol singers were there on that occasion - one might imagine them picking their way through the sad London streets before rebuilding had got under way. The music, though solemn, was enough to stir the nation to optimism and hope for a better future. The Festival was attended by their Majesties the King and Queen and was conducted by Sir Adrian Boult and Sir Malcolm Sargent. Works performed were 'Thanksgiving for Victory', for soprano solo, speaker, chorus and orchestra, by Ralph Vaughan Williams (Isobel Baillie, soprano); 'For the Fallen' from 'The Spirit of England' by Edward Elgar; and 'Blest Pair of Sirens' by C. Hubert Parry.

1958 saw the National Federation of Music Societies' Annual Conference in Bristol. The Bristol Choral Society, with the Bristol Cathedral Special Choir, Cheltenham Bach Choir and Stroud Choral Society, with the

Bournemouth Symphony Orchestra, gave a grand concert in the Colston Hall, conducted by Mr. Clifford Harker and Mr. Samuel Underwood.

Unfortunately, Mr. Underwood died in 1958. Society members paid great tribute to this gentleman - for his devoted service, working hard through the war years with innumerable problems. He had braved the blitz, travelling from Stroud to Bristol, and back, throughout a long period, which must have been exhausting with limited amounts of petrol. His place was taken that year by **Dr. W.K. Stanton** and his first concerts included 'A Sea Symphony' and 'Towards the Unknown Region' as a tribute to Ralph Vaughan Williams, who had died on the same day as Samuel Underwood. Elgar's 'Dream of Gerontius' was also one of the first works performed with Dr. Stanton, as a memorial to Mr. Underwood himself.

Dr. Stanton conducted six concerts only, before being taken seriously ill in 1960 and, having by now become one of the foremost conductors in the region, **Mr. Clifford Harker** was invited to undertake the planned programme for the remainder of the Society's season, 1960-61, with its current membership of 200.

The season included music already planned by Dr. Stanton - Elgar 'The Kingdom', Verdi 'Stabat Mater', Brahms 'German Requiem'. In November of that year Clifford was appointed permanent conductor - a happy relationship which lasted for twenty-nine years.

The business of the Choir was conducted by a loyal and efficient Committee, but Clifford had free rein with regard to the music performed, and always received the complete support and encouragement of the Chairman and Committee, who worked hard and constantly for the smooth running of everything concerned - rehearsals, welfare of members, music, and all concert arrangements. Concert dress for the ladies was a choice of either white or black evening dress, or white blouse and long black skirt. Gentlemen wore black tie evening dress.

Mr. Graham Harris was rehearsal accompanist when Clifford joined the Society. In 1966 he completed 50 years in this capacity, was succeeded by **Michael Dyer** that year.

Rehearsals continued at the Museum Lecture Theatre on Tuesdays at 7.15pm. Clifford made no revolutionary changes to the Society. He entered quietly and continued with the work started so many years before but it is highly likely that one particular innovation was welcomed by most people. That concerned the singing of the **National Anthem**. With the exception of Messiah, the National Anthem preceded all Bristol Choral Society concerts in the Colston Hall. Over the years, various arrangements were used, including the Britten version but by far the most popular (and inspiring) was Elgar's splendid arrangement; that is, Elgar, arr.C.H. Edward Elgar asked for a soprano solo in the first verse (two lines, repeated by the choir, throughout the verse) but arr.C.H. was to have a full four- part first verse. The substitution of the second verse was gladly welcomed by most people. The original second verse, quite archaic in its poetry, had caused many letters to the Press since Queen Victoria's day, (with its 'confound their politicks, frustrate their knavish tricks, etc.). Clifford's gentle but more appropriate substitution of 'God bless our native land, may heaven's protecting hand still guard our shore, etc.' became beloved of many and universally accepted as infinitely more suitable and far superior. The singing of the National Anthem, particularly Elgar's arrangement, made a magnificent beginning to a programme. As the conductor entered and mounted the rostrum there was a hush of expectancy. There came the signal to the drummer, who gave a drum-roll of considerable duration ending with an explosive crescendo, followed by the first few bars on the strings. It was an electrifying moment, by any standard. Remarks were often made that it was almost a concert in itself. There were always several minute's pause afterwards before the audience was settled and ready for the raised baton and the commencement of the first item.

The Society settled into a concert pattern of November, December (Messiah) and March, with the rehearsal venue changing to the Physics Lecture Theatre at the University in 1973. Clifford inspired new life into the Choir, enabling it to become a great choir, with high standards that never faltered at any time during Clifford's tenure.

Occasionally, there was a guest instrumental soloist - **Dr. Herbert Sumsion** came to play organ continuo in Messiah, the Beethoven Piano Concerto was played by **Nigel Coxe** in 1965; in 1967 the Colston Hall Centenary Concert included **Spivakovsky** playing the Brahms Violin Concerto; **Enid Clarke** played Franck's Symphonic Variations in 1968, and in 1971 she played the Dohnanyi 'Variations on a Nursery Theme'. In 1974, **Simon Preston** played in the Poulenc Organ Concerto; **Francis Jackson** (York Minster) played Handel's Organ Concerto No. 4 in 1979; **John Marsh** played the Handel Organ Concerto No. 2 in 1985; and in 1988, **Malcolm Binns** played the piano in Beethoven's Choral Fantasia.

Good rehearsal accompanists are rare creatures indeed, and **Michael Dyer** was greatly missed by the Society. **John Jenkins**, still at school, stepped in as accompanist at a moment's notice. These were very demanding works for all concerned but, for one as yet so inexperienced, John showed outstanding courage and skill as he persevered with the preparation. He had never accompanied a large choir before and, on his own admission, he was quite terrified at first, starting when the choir was part way through rehearsals of these difficult works, and the accompaniment was extremely difficult for him. Clifford showed him how to fiddle around with the accompaniment to make it playable - and it did. He admitted eventually that it was the best thing that had happened to him regarding accompanying as he proved to himself that he could do it! He never forgot the experience, but members of the choir greatly respected him for his noble efforts, and were always grateful to him for stepping in at such short notice. **Alistair Jones**, Director of Music at the Cathedral School, became permanent Accompanist in 1973 and the choir enjoyed his cheery and ebullient character. One most unfortunate occurrence, for Clifford, was an accident that happened whilst rehearsing The Kingdom, shortly before the concert in 1976. This resulted in a broken ankle and severe body strain. This brought Alistair to the forefront of Bristol music as he left the piano and became conductor for the remaining rehearsals and the concert. For him, it was a veritable initiation to be responsible for such a large affair, but he rose to the occasion most creditably and the choir supported him as he most capably and sensitively led choir and soloists through one of Elgar's greatest works. When Alistair left Bristol to work in London in 1978, **John Jenkins** became Accompanist until he left Bristol for a teaching appointment. **Martin Schellenberg** followed John in 1981 and, in 1983 **John Marsh** accompanied choir rehearsals until **Matthew Bale** took over from him in 1988.

It was a successful venture when the Choral Society combined with other choirs. This was infrequent but massed voices were really Clifford's forte and delight, and there was much goodwill between the choirs when they met together. In 1964 and 1979 there were performances of Bach's Mass in B minor with the Cathedral Special Choir, singers and orchestra numbering around 500, in the Colston Hall and, in 1969, a concert performance (in the Colston Hall) of Edward German's 'Merrie England' was given by these two choirs in the sweltering heat of a July day. This truly merrie performance was enlivened by well known Savoyards: **Valerie Masterson, Jean Allister, Thomas Round** and **Donald Adams**.

1972 brought the NFMS Annual Conference to Bristol and on that occasion the same two choirs joined forces for Elgar's Dream of Gerontius. In 1978, members sang in a chorus of 900 to give a mighty performance of Verdi's Requiem in the Royal Albert Hall, and in 1983 the Bristol Choral Society joined the Special Choir again, in the Cathedral, to give a summer programme of shorter works which included Handel's Zadok the Priest, Finzi's Lo, the Full Final Sacrifice and Parry's Blest Pair of Sirens.

Working with the choir in the second half of the twentieth century enabled Clifford to introduce music by modern composers, thus extending the previous repertoire. He certainly kept up with the times, as well as giving old favourites an airing from time to time. Works such as Tippett's Child of our Time, Walton's Belshazzar's Feast and Coronation Te Deum, Stravinsky's Symphony of Psalms, Poulenc's Gloria, Carl Orff's Carmina Burana, Holst's Hymn of Jesus, Kodaly's Psalmus Hungaricus, Missa Brevis, Te Deum, Britten's Spring Symphony and several works by Vaughan Williams not previously sung by the Society, were lapped up by choir and audience alike. A virtual new work was Malcolm Williamson's Mass of Christ the King (in its second performance), and a totally new work commissioned by the Society for the Choir's Centenary was Raymond Warren's Continuing Cities.

With Clifford Harker the Bristol Choral Society performed a wide variety of music, written by composers from the eighteenth century to the present day, old favourites being repeated at 'comfortable' intervals and, whilst much sacred music was performed, it was generally accepted that the great Passions were the prerogative of the Special Choir whilst Handel's Messiah was customary to the Choral Society. The only exception to this was in 1976 when the Choir sang Bach's St. Matthew Passion. Special occasions were eagerly anticipated; in 1967 the Colston Hall celebrated its Centenary and in a concert to mark this the Society performed Vaughan Williams' Five Mystical Songs with **John Carol-Case**. In 1972, the Society took part in the **Bristol Proms** season, singing Walton's Belshazzar's Feast, and joined with the Special Choir in a performance of Elgar's Dream of Gerontius at the NFMS Conference in Bristol that year.

November, 1980, saw an interesting programme when, in addition to Vaughan Williams' Five Mystical Songs and an orchestral item Elgar's Serenade, a new work 'Mass of Christ the King' by the Master of the Queen's Musick, Australian **Malcolm Williamson**, was performed. This was the first complete performance as writing of the work was not complete at the time of its first performance in London. Malcolm Williamson gave an interesting pre-concert talk on his new work at Bristol University, not only for students but for any choir member or audience who wished to attend. Difficulties in rehearsal had been experienced not only because the score was hardly complete but also the choir had to read from very quickly executed manuscript copies. The experience remained a talking point for a long time but, as always, Clifford had prepared carefully and with the choir he took rehearsals as if it was an 'old favourite' when, in fact, it was an exceedingly difficult score to read and interpret.

The programme was repeated in February, 1981, when the whole company, including the orchestra, visited the Brangwen Hall, Swansea. This occasion was not without incident: it was an extremely cold day with draughts everywhere, particularly in the changing rooms. The harpist did not arrive for rehearsal and, during the afternoon, a plaintive message was received from the railway station to say that she could not get a taxi that could carry her harp, so John Giddings offered to collect her with his vehicle in which he had transported his timps. The return journey was equally cold and snowy, with cold coaches threatening to break down through struggling against the fierce wind and snow. Fortunately, everyone eventually arrived back in Bristol none the worse, but very late and tired!

There was a diversion from the regular concert pattern in 1982, when the BBC's 'Much Loved Music Show' was televised from the Colston Hall. The Society was invited to take part in the programme with Elgar's 'As torrents in summer', Wagner's 'Hail, bright abode' (from Tannhäuser) and Fauré's 'Libera me' (from his Requiem). Clifford was asked by the BBC to train the choir for this event, which he agreed to with good grace, but he did not appear on the programme as the resident conductor of the series, **Owain Arwel Hughes**, took over at the Colston Hall.

In 1984, during the Messiah performance, Clifford was presented with a cheque from members (handed to him by the Lord Mayor and Lady Mayoress), to mark his **25th year** with the Society.

Two further concerts in the Bristol Proms series were given in 1986, when Vaughan Williams' Five Tudor Portraits and Carl Orff's Carmina Burana were performed and, in 1987, when Elgar's Dream of Gerontius was the work performed.

As the **Centenary** of the Society was approaching, several years' preparation was necessary for a grand celebration. The Centenary season opened in November, 1988, with a most enjoyable programme: Brahms' Academic Festival Overture, Puccini's Messa di Gloria, Beethoven's Choral Fantasia (with pianist Malcolm Binns) and Parry's Blest Pair of Sirens. In December the customary Messiah, and the Centenary Concert in April consisted of Elgar's The Music Makers and the commissioned work by Raymond Warren, Continuing Cities. Later in April a Centenary Dinner was held at the Grand Hotel, Bristol, also bidding farewell to Clifford, and in June an informal evening was held at the Scotch Horn, Nailsea, at which members entertained each other - exposing much personal talent hitherto unknown, ranging between a poetic adulation to Clifford, and very jolly pieces played on a concertina. Clifford was surprised and amused to listen to a group of BCS singers presenting a youthful arr.C.H. in the form of 'The Owl and the Pussycat', and to the great delight of everyone present.

In July a gala G&S evening was held at the Colston Hall, Clifford at his merry best, when everyone enjoyed singing through 'Trial by Jury' and excerpts from 'The Gondoliers'. This was a thoroughly enjoyable occasion, though bitter-sweet, for it was Clifford's last concert with the Society and afterwards there were many pangs of sadness, members trying to put this moment out of their minds until it actually happened. Bristol Choral Society bade farewell to its much-loved Director of Music, knowing they had lost a very special person.

Looking back over the twenty-nine years that Clifford had shared with Bristol Choral Society, people remembered him with tremendous admiration and affection. To most members, Tuesday choral rehearsals with him were the highlight of the week, whilst concerts were truly unforgettable occasions, to be treasured for the remainder of peoples' lives. Rehearsals meant hard work, but made more than enjoyable by this great man, by his methods, personality, humour, and ways of obtaining positive results from his flawless coaching.

He had always been quick to notice choir numbers at rehearsal. Should there be less people than normal, he would ask "Where is everyone?" When told "Half Term" he would give his typical loud cry "Ha!" (which was really a half-laugh) and then the baton would come down. Very occasionally, after the November concert, to him there would seem to be more people than usual. Then he would ask "Where has everyone come from?" giving his knowing, wry smile. These extra numbers were more likely because there were so few Messiah rehearsals and no-one wanted to miss, rather than from disinterest in other music.

Rehearsals had been extremely interesting; Clifford would be so well acquainted with the works that he would talk about them, giving background information, illustrating the musical writing on the piano and generally enthusing over the pieces - and all for the better enjoyment of the works, without labouring anything. He would tell the choir about soloists he had engaged for the concerts, and interesting anecdotes seemed to come naturally from him. His own musicality had shone through when, at one rehearsal, someone moved a chair which screeched on the floor. At once, Clifford said That's a B flat" (or whatever it was), and promptly went to the piano and played the note in question.

At the end of one rehearsal Clifford announced that he would like to make a few temporary changes to the seating of some parts of the choir, relating to the work being prepared. He said he knew this was a dangerous thing to do (as he knew people liked their own 'place') but, typically, he made a joke of the whole matter by telling the choir about a lady who, when asked to move for a similar reason declared "I have been here since The Creation and I shall remain here until the Amen." This affected the desired 'move' without the slightest bother.

It remained part of Clifford's charm and sensitivity that, although people were auditioned for entry into the Choir, despite occasional suggestions that members should be re-auditioned after a time, he always refused to do so. He did not relish a re-selection process whereby certain people would need to be excluded, people who, maybe, were not able to contribute the same quality voices as once they could. But it was these very people to whom the Society gave great pleasure; they had supported the choir for most of their lives, many of them, and brought along their friends to concerts and were great sellers of tickets. These remained the backbone of the Society and although Clifford knew he carried a few 'passengers', he also knew that no voice stood out to mar the effect of the whole, and was content to know that the many good voices made up for what was lacking in some.

No eulogy to Clifford and his choirs would be complete without particular mention of two attributes; the first relating to his performances of **Handel's Messiah** - how he made every rendering a moving experience for all those involved, drawing out the spirituality of the work which is the very essence of the Christian faith. His interpretation was imbued with a humanity that seemed to make the work his own. Since his youth he had loved the work, that being evident in his keenness to perform it in Cairo under wartime conditions. After this he continued the tradition of Bristol Choral Society by giving what surely amounted to hundreds of performances of this mighty work, most of them being with this Society. Members looked forward to this annual event which, together with a most regular and appreciative audience, was the commencement of Christmas for a great many people. It had long been the custom of the Society to give a performance on the Saturday previous to Christmas Day, and when Clifford's personality was infused into the work an atmosphere of uplifting and reverence, the Colston Hall was always packed to capacity. By 1973 it became necessary to use the Saturday previous, in addition, in order to satisfy the crowds who wanted to hear the work. It was always a thrill to see the sign 'House Full' as members arrived for the concert, and to see the look of eager anticipation on people's faces as they mounted the steps to the Hall. From an entirely commercial point of view, full houses meant the topping up of the Society's coffers enabling them to afford first rate soloists and large orchestras for the more expensive programmes. But the popularity of Messiah remained the key reason for performing the work annually. In Clifford's earlier years coach loads of people would travel from Wales and further afield to listen to his rendering, and the area around the Hall would be simply teaming with a vast throng of eager concert-goers. When a new concert hall was built in Cardiff the Welsh naturally supported their own, but the Colston Hall would still be packed to capacity on the two Messiah nights. Sometimes Press comments can be hard-hitting and Clifford's speed was called to question in one report of a Messiah. True, some choruses were less stately than of yore and could even be described as taken at a cracking pace. But Clifford knew what he was doing, and he knew his text; therefore to take 'All we like sheep' along at a sprightly pace was to him fully descriptive of the silly sheep, scattering in all directions, not knowing where to turn nor whom to follow. At the same time it must be stated that his speed was always consistent and a fast pace never got out of control. Clifford's influence on sacred works was such that he could create a reverent atmosphere from the very first note and the work would unfold in a remarkably convincing way. This was true, not only of Messiah, but whenever Messiah was being performed Clifford requested that there be no applause at the Interval, and afterwards the work continued with the same composure.

Clifford's Messiah rehearsals were surely unique. It seems that the work is never done in its entirety, but once it was decided to perform it on two nights, it did make it possible to cover most choruses (and solos) by excluding some and including others over the two evenings. However, on the first Messiah rehearsal evening it was a delight to see the pleasure in Clifford's face as he tapped his stick for the beginning. He would beam over to his right, saying "page five, altos, 'And the Glory'" and with his usual aplomb, another Clifford experience was off to a lively start. Most choruses were covered during the few weeks available for refreshing one's memory but it was always a big surprise to anyone singing Messiah for the first time, who had to learn as best they could, as sometimes choruses were not sung in their entirety and the Hallelujah Chorus was always sung from memory.

It was not until the evening performance that Messiah really came alive. The afternoon rehearsal (on the first Saturday only) was what one could describe only as an amusing experience. Two o'clock prompt start and **maybe** the whole of the Overture but, after that, choruses, recitatives and arias were just 'touched' - a few bars and then on to the next item. Clifford had honed and polished his own version of the work, and stuck to it through

26. Bristol Choral Society 'Messiah' in Colston Hall, Bristol, December 1987.

thick and thin. For instance, woe betide any up-and-coming young soloist who thought they were going to take 'their' arias at 'their' speeds. Even if he agreed to take it at their speed it usually eventually settled into his! Although Messiah rehearsals were typically similar, the performance **never** suffered - Clifford was confident in the complete response he would receive from all performers. And each performance was a gem, alive and vibrant. He prepared his Messiah, as all his work, with the knowledge that what had not been learned by the Saturday two-hour rehearsal could not be changed. All the same, his choir was well prepared before the day of the performance.

Saturday afternoon rehearsals were not without their amusing incidents. If the rehearsal started a little sluggishly, he would look up and say "What's the matter with you?" Then, as he once again looked down to his score, with a half smile he would remark "You've been eating too many jam butties." Once, the solo trumpet was not at the rehearsal and the orchestra leader, then Edwin Brown, was asked to play the trumpet line of 'A trumpet shall sound' on his violin so that the aria could be rehearsed. When the soloist came in he sang out, without the slightest flinch and with great thrust "The violin shall sound....." There was so much laughter that it brought the rehearsal to a temporary halt.

Amusing incidents were always happening at both rehearsal and concert, proving Clifford's ability to work hard yet keep the choir and orchestra relaxed in mood, which brought about the natural and happy atmosphere necessary for success.

The second attribute was Clifford's great love for **Edward Elgar's** music, which he championed all his life. He was a formidable Elgarian, and mention has already been made of this fact, but his affinity with this great music shone through whenever Elgar's works were being performed. He did not perform the composer too frequently, or more than any other, but the pleasure was obvious whenever he planned a programme to include Elgar. The magnificent 'Dream of Gerontius' was, to him, the ultimate experience but whenever The Kingdom or The Apostles were in rehearsal, his pleasure knew no bounds. He grasped Elgar's profound correlation between texts and musical expression and he became one of the foremost exponents of Elgar's music. His faithful interpretation was transmitted to his choirs and for these works soloists were chosen with even greater care. His audiences will long remember the spiritual atmosphere he created in Elgar's great choral works.

Whenever an Elgar piece was on the season's programme Clifford was particularly delighted to point out how the composer had translated words or feelings into sounds, creating some ecstatic moments, the greatest (it is believed) being the point in The Dream when the Soul is allowed a brief glimpse of God. There are heart-rending chords leading to a tremendous explosion of sound, unbelievably conceived by Elgar, generating many seconds' pause before any attempt to continue the drama. There were other instances where poignant 'moments' and ideas were explained which gave meaning to people's understanding of the piece, and in works like The Music

Makers, (to some not as great a composition as others of Elgar's) he loved to make comments with piano illustrations indicating the composer's quoting of his own musical themes in other works, and it all just came to life.

Bath Choral Society (1963-1988)

As with Bristol Choral Society, Bath was a well-established choir of some standing when Clifford was invited to become its Musical Director in 1963, and for twenty-five years he was beloved of both choir and audience.

Clifford already had a busy schedule, with the Cathedral, the Special Choir and Bristol Choral Society claiming much of his time, yet he gladly accepted the invitation to become permanent conductor of this Society, which averaged 100 singers.

Prior to Clifford's arrival the Director of Music was **William Jackman**, but when he became ill Clifford was invited as guest conductor for several concerts, becoming permanent Director of Music in November, 1964. In fact, he used to refer to Wednesday as his 'Bath night'. Rehearsals were held at the Friends' Meeting House in York Street, moving to Manvers Street Baptist Church about the end of the Seventies.

Michael Dyer went with Clifford each week to the rehearsals from the beginning, until 1970, then **John Jenkins** accompanied the choir for a time and was succeeded by **Stephen Taylor**.

The first concert conducted by Clifford was a rather special occasion, being the 80th birthday celebration of composer **George Dyson**, who was Patron of the Society for many years. Dyson's 'Canterbury Pilgrims' was performed on that occasion. After that, the Society performed a great variety of works which brought much appreciation from performers, orchestra, and audience alike. Works included Bach: Mass in B Minor, Elgar: The Dream of Gerontius, Mendelssohn: Elijah, Haydn: The Creation, Rossini: Petite Messe Solennelle, Vaughan Williams: Five Tudor Portraits, Handel: Acis and Galatea, Verdi: Requiem, and, of course, Handel: Messiah.

Bath Abbey was an excellent situation in which to perform the glorious Messiah. Clifford never tired of it, neither did the people of Bath and, by 1975 two performances in December were given in order to meet the demands of eager Bath audiences. At more than one performance of Messiah spontaneous applause broke out, at a time when such expressions of appreciation were not entirely welcome in the Abbey.

Most concerts were held in Bath Abbey, and one very exciting event was in 1973 when a Gala Concert was given to mark the 1000th Anniversary of the Crowning of King Edgar in the Abbey. In that concert Clifford himself was piano soloist, playing Mozart's Coronation Concerto.

Occasionally, a concert was given in the Pavilion; Mendelssohn's Elijah was performed there and several Gilbert and Sullivan concert performances were given with principals from the D'Oyley Carte Opera Company - Donald Adams, John Reid and Thomas Round.

Every summer there was an evening when lighter pieces were sung. The venue was St. Luke's Church, and guest performers would include a brass or string quartet. The concerts were followed by cheese and wine.

Another special event occurred during Clifford's period when the Society commemorated its Centenary in 1982. Celebrations during that season included a Summer Concert held at Prior Park College when the Choir sang Fauré's Requiem in the Chapel there, and gave a memorable performance of Verdi's Requiem.

Stephen Taylor, an ex-chorister and an organ pupil at Bristol Cathedral followed John Jenkins as Choir Accompanist and, again, he would travel with Clifford each Wednesday by train. On the way from the station a customary glass of sherry was taken, and so the pair would arrive well prepared for the evening's music. Stephen remembered rehearsing the Verdi Requiem particularly because of the accompaniment which in some places contained 8-part fugues, and he found it very difficult to read the score **and** help the voices with their entries.

All Clifford's accompanists were competent musicians, in whom he placed all his trust, and they never failed him or his choirs. **Robin Walker** followed Stephen in 1971 until 1979. John Jenkins returned until 1981, being succeeded by Martin Schellenberg from 1981 until 1987, when **Matthew Bale** became the Choir's official Accompanist.

There were many social events for choir members to enjoy, in addition to their choral concerts. The organising committee kept everyone happy by arranging barn dances, skittles matches, river and canal cruises, and musical events held in the Octagon in Milsom Street. An annual 'Money for Music' day was held in the Pavilion when all music societies in Bath were invited to have stands for their own funds. Bath Choral Society usually undertook to provide refreshments throughout the day - 7.30 a.m. Breakfast, followed by coffee, lunches and afternoon tea - but never on a concert day!

In 1988 the Choir commenced rehearsals for a well-loved work, Elgar's The Kingdom. During rehearsals for this Clifford announced that he was to retire from the Choir after that performance. It was a sad time, but the Choir gave a memorable performance, one of Clifford's favourites, and so the musical partnership came to an end.

A Farewell Dinner was given for Clifford just prior to his retirement, when he was pleased to learn that his good friend, **Matthew Bale**, in whom he had such great confidence and whom he held in high regard, was going to succeed him as Musical Director.

An Appreciation in the programme of The Kingdom expressed in words the feelings that every member held for Clifford:

'In all that he has touched Mr. Clifford Harker brought to bear
his excellent musicianship, his detailed knowledge of a very
wide range of music, and consistently convincing realisations of
the printed score into living music. Not least among his
achievements have been the assembly of as fine an orchestra as

any choral society could desire and his selection of excellent soloists, many of whom have become singers of national repute. Clifford Harker has served the Society for a quarter of a century and will long be remembered with great affection.'

Lord Mayor's Chapel Choir (1984 - 1996)

The invitation to become Organist and Choirmaster at St. Mark's, the Lord Mayor's Chapel on College Green, Bristol, came just at the right moment for Clifford. Retirement from all that he had been accustomed to doing at the Cathedral had not come easy to him, even though he still had the enjoyment of his Bath and Bristol Choral Societies. He sorely missed the regularity of services and of 'belonging' to a place of worship. Most of all he missed the organ and choral music for which he had been responsible for so many years.

Therefore, the Lord Mayor's Chapel post was ideal. It was a small and beautiful place, and gave him back something of what he was missing, keeping him alert and active for a good few years. He had a happy association with the Archdeacon, Rev. Leslie Williams, who had presided at the Chapel since 1968, together with the small choir and officials who kept the Chapel running.

There was a devotional Service every Sunday morning (attended by thirty to forty people) except in August, for which music was to be prepared, and choir rehearsed, and Clifford made certain that everything on the musical side was ready and well prepared.

The Choir was as loyal as any, a number of members having been in the Choir for twenty or so years, and all were capable and well qualified to sing the services on the Lord's Day. The eight-strong choir rehearsed on Thursday evening fortnightly and if a member was unable to sing on any Sunday they were responsible for providing an approved substitute, who also attended the appropriate rehearsal.

Services took the form of the customary Anglican sung Mattins and sung Eucharist; there were Psalms to prepare, and short anthems, motets and seasonal music by a large number of composers. Clifford's careful co-operation over the planning of Services ensured that suitable music was sung, and once more his skills with small ensembles came into play, with his good choice of suitable anthems and some of his own arrangements in addition to the occasional inclusion of his own Communion Service. There was also the regular use of an AMEN, written specially for the Lord Mayor's Chapel Choir, always referred to as the 'Dingles Amen', reminding Clifford of the day he put it together whilst sipping tea in Dingles restaurant. The National Anthem was sung each Sunday. Thus he was glad to be still serving in the Lord's House, even on a less grand scale, and was quite at home in the situation, processing through the Chapel, quite unpretentious in his gown, with the robed choir.

The Lord Mayor's Chapel was well used; for many years the boys of Queen Elizabeth's Hospital School held their Morning Service at 10 a.m., prior to the public Service at 11 a.m. on Sundays. During the Church Year there was pageantry in miniature when, in addition to normal Sunday services, at one time (though not whilst Clifford was there), the Assize Courts held a Service at the beginning of their sessions. There was also a Service (at which the QEH Choir sang) after the Mayor-Making Ceremony at the Council House. Clifford also played the organ for Council Prayers when a new Council was installed. Organisations such as the Bristol Savages and Soroptomists also held an annual service there. Occasionally there would be a wedding.

Always there were events like these to prepare for and to keep Clifford on his toes. In addition, the Choir always sang carols one evening before Christmas to the Lord Mayor and his party at the Mansion House.

During the summer the Choir and guests enjoyed social outings which was generally an excellent supper at a country venue.

Graham Hooper, who had been organist at the Lord Mayor's Chapel for many years, was a close associate of Clifford's. He had retired in 1975 and **Dr. Nigel Davison** was organist between 1976 and 1978, and **Malcolm Harding** (1971-1981) and **Malcolm Riley** (1982-1984) followed on. Clifford remained as organist for twelve years, from 1984 until 1996.

He was often to be found at the Chapel. He enjoyed the organ and, with **Alan Canterbury** (verger) took pleasure in talking with visitors who went in to admire the lovely gem of a church. There were regular recitals, given by instrumental ensembles, singers, and organists, on Saturday afternoons. Clifford was glad to arrange these events and was there every time, ready to talk to people in the audience, always announcing the next recital.

As his health began to give problems and he found it difficult to travel down to the Chapel, he thought it prudent not to continue at the Lord Mayor's Chapel and so, after a happy time of less stressful responsibilities, he finally and quietly passed into full retirement.

The Orchestras

Clifford Harker's orchestras are mentioned last - not at all because they are least important - but to the contrary; they were a fine body of people, hand picked for their competence and reliability. Most players took part in the concerts of all three large societies and, under Clifford, performed a great variety of music.

In his early days in Bristol Clifford formed a small orchestra to play in concerts given by the Madrigal Society and these players were to become the nucleus of his Special Choir Orchestra.

This orchestra comprised both good amateurs and professional musicians. Nowadays, this might be undiplomatic to arrange, but at the time it was an accepted situation and it worked well for Clifford and players. The

27. The Lord Mayor's Chapel Choir.

only time it became a matter of delicate diplomacy was at the rehearsal, payment being made to the professionals playing for Musicians' Union rates, whilst amateurs played for nothing. **Gerry Nichols** was asked by **Sydney Carter** (Treasurer of the Special Choir) to help him with this task which proved somewhat worrying at first, but he quickly learned who was who, thus saving himself, and the players, much embarrassment. It was, however, clear evidence of Clifford's personality and musical standards that such a mixture could work and enjoy music together.

Edwin Brown was a well known Bristol violinist and was Leader of Colston Hall orchestras well before Clifford's arrival, and was greatly respected and valued by Clifford until his retirement in 1966. He had taken on the responsibility of 'fixer' - the person who assembled the required number of players for a particular programme. Clifford showed much faith in the players he engaged but after he retired Clifford undertook his own 'fixing'.

After Edwin Brown, **George Budden** became Leader, followed by **Antony Pooley**, who led for a long time up to Clifford's retirement. It was Antony who jokingly asserted that the leader's job was to mow a path and give the conductor an unobstructed way to the rostrum. He remembered Clifford with great pleasure and also felt that anyone who could coax, cajole, or even will, an orchestra in one rehearsal for works like The Apostles, The Kingdom, Psalmus Hungaricus, (and many other works could be cited here) must be a very special sort of person. He retained the thrill of working with Clifford - he was a conductor in a million - he remembered the magnificent carols 'arr.C.H.', and felt that many people received as much pleasure from Carol concerts as from the big works.

Clifford's invitation to 'good amateur players' was unquestionably magnanimous but, as always, he made wise choices. His good friend, **John Bennett** would travel from Northampton to play in Cathedral concerts for a number of years, and **Enid Hunt** played violin for him from the beginning - in Madrigal Society concerts and in Special Choir concerts for a long time.

It was Enid Hunt who explained that in the early days string players were voluntary and Clifford would find time to hold rehearsals on three Thursday evenings before a concert was due. Then the whole orchestra assembled for an afternoon rehearsal on the Friday of the concert. Proof of the orchestra's competence is evident in the Press report of the first Special Choir concert:

> 'In the spacious, kindly acoustic of a cathedral it is difficult to judge the quality of an orchestra but Mr. Harker seemed to have assembled an ample and accomplished group of instrumentalists and they gave him noble support.'

Orchestras respected Clifford for his concise, efficient rehearsals. (There were a few exceptions, apparently, when Beethoven's Ninth Symphony was being prepared, and some twentieth century works). Everything was produced in one three-hour rehearsal - a feat that remains quite incredible in most people's opinion. Nevertheless, he always started on time and stopped on the dot, keeping good time at rehearsals, and it was amazing that he was able to cohere an orchestra on one rehearsal.

From his players Clifford gained much admiration and respect, many of them staying in his orchestras for a good number of years, and he was fondly regarded both for his conducting of many different styles of music and as an imaginative arranger of Christmas Carols. They felt it a joy to be 'under his baton', enjoying competent but not over-long rehearsals, especially for Messiah. Some players would play Messiah four or five times for Clifford alone and in all those years of Messiah-playing for him, members of the orchestra felt they could have done a whole performance without him, but doing it exactly as if he was there.

Margaret and **John Wills** (cello and double-bass) played for Clifford between 1972 and 1989. They were both constantly impressed by his efficiency - he unfailingly sent out their contracts, usually in May, for a year ahead for the three choral societies. That gave them all details needed, which was greatly appreciated,

'In rehearsal, players found he was efficient without being officious. He would not tolerate incompetence - musical or otherwise - or unpunctuality in any player whatsoever. For this he gained the respect of his players. He was always so courteous, with an old-worldly charm and great charisma, impeccably dressed, and there was always a grandeur about his performance.'

Similar sentiments were expressed by a number of regular players.

David Mason, who played solo trumpet for Clifford for many years up to the time Clifford retired (possibly forty years), was based in London and was one of the country's leading trumpet players. He found Clifford professional, relaxed and helpful. He missed only one Messiah and that was because he was held up on the motorway for seven hours due to an accident. He never attended rehearsals, having to travel from London, but this was accepted and he would always seek out Clifford well before the beginning of the concert to let him know that he had arrived.

When his regular orchestra was augmented instrumentalists immediately recognised Clifford's ability. On one occasion, some visiting BBC brass players had been engaged for a concert in the Colston Hall. During the rehearsal one of them sitting near **John Giddings** leaned over and asked him who the conductor was. On being told, the player replied "He's wonderful; far better than some of the people we have to work with."

John Giddings was first introduced to the Bristol Choral Society in 1957 as timpanist, after Reg. Hibbins, who was a member of the BBC West of England Light Orchestra. He was soon playing in all three of Clifford's choirs and found Clifford a superb conductor to work with. Clifford was able to get what he wanted with little apparent effort - no mean achievement on only one rehearsal and an *ad hoc* orchestra. His sense of humour, relaxed manner and great charm were attributes too often absent with some conductors. But Clifford did his homework well! This was apparent during full rehearsals, as he knew what he needed the most and least of the rehearsal time. This became evident to John when the Bristol Choral Society performed Beethoven's Ninth Symphony on only one full rehearsal in 1980. (This was one of the few works that did, in fact, require a little more rehearsal). In comparison, as a free-lance player, John had done some work with the BBC Training Orchestra as an 'extra', under various conductors. At that time they rehearsed for a whole week for a one-hour recorded programme containing standard repertoire items.

Gradually, Clifford's orchestras became totally professional. Even then, adequate rehearsal was required for the players drawn mainly from professional players living in Bristol or nearby. It was his custom to obtain the hired orchestral parts and issue them to the players in good time, which was appreciated. He was helped with this task by a choir member - one of the many 'behind the scenes' tasks to be done - who collected the parts from Clifford, with names and addresses clipped to the appropriate parts, posted or delivered them by hand, and collected them in again after the concert, handing them back to Clifford for return. This was a great help to the conductor and was evidence of his meticulous organisational practices. John Hilton did this small job for Bristol Choral Society for many years. There were many small but essential jobs to be done to ensure that all concert arrangements were completed, which John did, even to putting out the music stands. This was a job shunned by a lot of folk because they were awkward and fiddly with a mind of their own, but putting them out and then replacing them in their special box after concerts was one thing to be done in order to leave the Hall in a tidy state.

There were anxious moments, occasionally, on the part of the players. Once, when rehearsing Vaughan Williams' Sea Symphony one Saturday afternoon, Clifford, always anxious not to override MU rules, put down his baton at 5.30 pm prompt, and said "Well, that's it, we have run out of time, go home and have your tea." After a silence of a few seconds, the leader said "But we have not done the last movement yet." Clifford replied "I know. Watch me tonight and everything will be all right." The entire programme went well. This was a prime example of the old adage 'It will be all right on the night'!

It was well known that rehearsals with Clifford were rather jolly occasions - a tense rehearsal will often benefit from a well-timed touch of humour. This fact, John Giddings remembered, was demonstrated by the principal percussionist, Paul Chalklin, at one afternoon rehearsal with the orchestra. One particular work being performed contained a part for a tam-tam (or large gong). Paul possessed a vast amount of percussion equipment and on that occasion he had brought along his largest tam-tam, about five feet in diameter. At the correct place he gave the instrument the required stroke. The sound was awe-inspiring. When the reverberations finally died down there was a deathly silence. Clifford looked towards the source of the sound and said "But it's only a quaver, Mr. Chalklin." The laughter and applause from the assembled was tumultuous!

It was not only Special Choir members who loved the carol arrangements. So did the orchestra, and John Giddings found that the timpani parts were a delight to play. He thought that Clifford wrote well for his instrument and was proud to say that, without hesitation, he felt that Clifford's timpani parts surpassed those written by other specialist arrangers. Maybe it was due to Clifford's own experience with the instrument that he could write so well for it. Only a few people knew that at the Royal College of Music he was required to play a third instrument - and Clifford chose the timpani. He confided to Lionel Pike once that when playing in an orchestra he could not hear to tune the drums to a different note, so he would quietly ask a trombonist, or someone nearby, to give him the note.

Clifford was remembered by all his players as a real gentleman and musician of a high order, who brought so much enjoyment and achievement within the experience of so many people. **Stewart McKim** (double bass) recalled one occasion when, at one afternoon rehearsal, one of the players was in difficulty. He spoke up: "Every time the baritone soloist stands up he blocks my view and I can't see the beat." He then added the fateful words "Not that it matters!" Such an indiscretion would have occasioned an explosion from an authoritarian individual, but Clifford merely smiled quietly, and the necessary seat adjustments were made.

Stewart emphasised that Clifford never wasted time in rehearsal. After a very few bars of the Hallelujah Chorus, he would stop. "Well, we know this, don't we?" and would move on to the next number. If a rehearsal ended early as a result he never worried, and everyone was relieved to conserve forces for the performance. But heaven help the player who came late at the start! One player in particular was becoming quite well known for cutting it fine, dashing in at the last minute, always with very plausible excuses - the traffic, dreadful parking, etc. etc. When he finally turned up substantially late one afternoon he was told he should start setting out in good time or his services would no longer be required. This effected an immediate cure.

Generally, though, Clifford was very loyal to players, asking them back season after season, and there was a very good feeling in the band. However, he did expect loyalty, and should a player ring up to cancel a contract (in the hope of getting more money elsewhere) he could be sure he would not be asked again.

John Dixon (cello) had a splendid time playing for Clifford in all his orchestras from 1965 until Clifford retired. He, too, found him meticulous in organisation, and courteous, and he had no doubt about the great man's sincerity. He was particularly impressed by Clifford's attention to the finer details of performance. If a soloist was unable to appear, Clifford always announced it himself, introducing and welcoming the substitute soloist. He noticed, too, that Clifford always kept his eye on a solo player (a point which

Jim Gowers (bassoon) made in his reminiscences, when he said that Clifford always gave one a glance just before a solo entry - "musically, he would give you room, so to speak, to play the solo as you wanted to.").

John Dixon was most thoughtful towards Clifford. Knowing that it was not easy to get to the Colston Hall, especially on a Saturday afternoon, he would collect Clifford from his home for the rehearsal and for the concert in the Colston Hall. He used to give Clifford a bottle of gin at Christmas and, on thanking him, Clifford would remark with a twinkle in his eye "No gin before a concert, eh!"

During the time that Clifford was organist at the Lord Mayor's Chapel John Dixon (who played in the Dorian Quartet with George Lang, Richard Thorn and Helen Goodman) gave recitals in Clifford's Saturday afternoon programmes. Clifford always sent him a Christmas Card from the Chapel, adding the words 'Happy Memories' in his own distinctive handwriting.

To many listeners it was a delight to discover how Clifford achieved the best possible effects from the instruments. **Roger Crudge** vividly remembered one rehearsal for a lighter work, 'Merrie England', when the effects of certain instruments were not to Clifford's satisfaction. He stopped the orchestra and suggested that the flutes played in a certain way, and another section played in a different way, all this having the effect of transforming the sound completely. It made Roger realise just how vital a good conductor was to anyone's music making.

Without any doubt, people who played under Clifford realised, and truly valued, having him in Bristol - his beat was so clear and expressive. He was undoubtedly totally secure in all he did.

....

CHAPTER 5
CHURCHES, ORGANS, RECITALS
'You shall teach us your song's new numbers'

St. George's Church, Jesmond, Newcastle upon Tyne

The first organ that Clifford had the chance to play would undoubtedly be on home ground - in the beautiful church of St. George's, Jesmond, where he spent his formative years.

Both church and organ were interesting in their initiation. In 1887, Newcastle staged a great Exhibition as a means of promoting and advertising the many engineering and industrial skills found in the region at that period. George Mitchell, a ship builder on the Tyne, and who lived at Jesmond Towers, paid for the building of the church, hall and vicarage giving, also, the site. He undertook to pay for everything, right down to the hymn books. The architect, Thomas R. Spence was engaged and Mitchell insisted that no expense be spared in the construction and ornamentation of the church. His son, Charles William Mitchell, was responsible for some of the fine interior decoration, which is in the *art nouveau* style. On entering the church the impression given is that of a small cathedral with a long nave and painted roof. The floors throughout the building are laid with fine mosaics set with Christian symbols, which can also be found, along with a flower theme, in the walls, floor, ceilings, woodwork and glass. The beautiful stained glass windows are mainly Spence and range from a comparatively plain style to rich and colourful patterns. The seven windows of the south aisle contain a dog calendar, a mediaeval device used to indicate the passing of the year where no clock was available.

Externally, St. George's, though Victorian, is as attractive as any in the early English style, and stands well at the end of its broad church green. Its tower, 154 feet high, containing a ring of eight bells, is a bold interpretation of the campanile of St' Mark's, Venice, and the fine ironwork of the main entrance gates not only bear testimony to the quality of workmanship, but impart this message to worshippers: 'Do all to the Glory of God'.

Mitchell was well known amongst the industrialists of the time and he hit upon the idea of exhibiting the organ (which he had paid for) at the Exhibition. Recitals were given whilst the organ was on show, and amongst the organists was James M. Preston, who became the first organist of the new church.

The four manual organ was built by Messrs. T. C. Lewis & Co., of London, and in use before the church was completed (at the Exhibition) and a complimentary description of the instrument was recorded in the catalogue of a special loan collection at the Exhibition of 1887:

> '**Grand Organ**:- The Executive Council and the public are
> indebted to C. Mitchell Esq., for the use of the large Organ

28. Interior of St. George's Jesmond, Newcastle.

which has been erected here by Messrs. T. C. Lewis & Co., of London.

The organ is intended for presentation to St. George's Church, Jesmond, but as that building is at present only in progress, and will not be finished for some months, the munificent donor hastened the completion of the Organ, in order that it might be temporarily placed here, in the anticipation that it would add to the attraction of the Exhibition, an act of kindly thoughtfulness which will without doubt be well appreciated by the thousands of visitors who will find pleasure in listening to the instrument.

The character of Mr. Lewis's work is well-known in this district and throughout the northern counties, and the "countryman of the north" may remember with pride and satisfaction that they were the first to recognise the merit of his productions, when in the south his name was almost unknown; to this day they continue to support their choice, and in the magnificent Organ in the Cathedral Church of St. Nicholas possess one of the latest, as also one of the finest specimens of this builder's powerful command of the resources of his art. The Organ for Jesmond Church, although much smaller in its proportions, is not beneath our Cathedral Organ in its beauty, and the balance of tone. The specification having been drawn up in view of the Church purposes which the instrument was intended to serve, the Organ is necessarily laid out as a Church Organ, yet so bright, vigorous, and resonant are its tones, so rich, varied, and charming are its combinations, so life-like and orchestral many of its qualities of sound, that it is fully capable of rendering the music suitable to the concert-room in an efficient manner, and of taking part in public festivity.

A notable feature of the construction of the Organ is in its exhibiting a reversion to the older type of organ-building, which, in the modern increasing rage of fashion for pneumatic action, whether necessary or not, seemed almost to be passing away. The Organ stands square in its build, its action is direct tracker action without complication, its touch is crisp and free, space ample, regulation in detail easy, and by exactitude in work and arrangement, the wear and tear is reduced to a minimum; consequently this instance of reversion is a matter of common sense. The builder has not been hampered by any architectural restrictions, and therefore pneumatics are needless work; the cost they would have entailed has been better allotted to increasing the value of the instrument in other ways.'

The 'reversion to the older type of organ-building' referred to the method of giving power to the instrument - it was powered by a water-driven system designed by Mitchell's partner, Lord Armstrong, and remained an efficient system until new adaptations were made in the late 1930s. Clifford would have played the organ in its original specification.

Organ Specification

Three Manuals and Pedals. 34 Stops.

CHOIR ORGAN, CC to A, 58 notes.

Salicional	8 feet	Voix Celestes (tenC)	8 feet
Dulciana	8 feet	Geigen Principal	4 feet
Lieblich Gedact	8 feet	Horn	8 feet
Flauto Traverso	4 feet	Oboe	8 feet
Clarionet	8 feet	Vox Humana	8 feet

PEDAL ORGAN, CCC to F, 30 notes

GREAT ORGAN, CC to A, 58 notes

Bourdon	16 feet	Open Bass	16 feet
Open Diapason, No.1	8 feet	Violone (metal)	16 feet
Open Diapason No. 2	8 feet	Sub Bass	16 feet
Flûte Harmonique	8 feet	Bass Flute	8 feet
Octave	4 feet	Trombone	16 feet

COUPLERS.

Octave Quint	2²/3 feet	Choir to Pedal
Super Octave	2 feet	Great to Pedal
Mixture 4 ranks	1¹/3 feet	Swell to Pedal
Trumpet	8 feet	Swell to Great

SWELL ORGAN, CC toA, 58 notes. Swell to Choir

Lieblich Bourdon	16 feet	Six Pedals of Combination
Geigen Principal	8 feet	Great to Pedal on and off.
Rohr Flute	8 feet	Tremulant.
Viole de Gambe	8 feet	

Cathedral Church of St. Nicholas, Newcastle upon Tyne

Apart from the organs that were played during his educational training, i.e. at the Royal College of Music and the Royal College of Organists, the next organs to be explored would be the organs of Newcastle Cathedral, where Clifford was sub-Organist from 1935 to 1939. As already mentioned above, the magnificent Grand Organ was built by **T. C. Lewis**, begun in 1881 and completed as a four-manual in 1891. It was contained within the cases of the **Renatus Harris** instrument of 1676. Contemporary writers remarked on the Diapasons as 'very fine', the Reeds and Mixtures 'extremely brilliant', and the Flutes 'equal to those of Schultz; the voicing 'producing' the best effects of the English, German and French schools of organ building.

When Clifford played this instrument in the 1930s there had been some modifications over the years but, during the instrument's centenary (1981) Messrs. Nicholson & Co. (Worcester) Ltd. , of Malvern, completely rebuilt it. This included structural re-planning of Divisions, redesigned wind supplies of a lower pressure, new electrical transmission, and improved tonal reflection of sound into the Cathedral, together with improvements to the appearance of the main case and an additional (mobile) Nave Console.

29. The organ of Newcastle Cathedral.

Organ Specification

Specification, after 1981 rebuilding:
MAIN CONSOLE (4 manual; drawstops)

LEFT JAMB

SWELL
1. Tremulant
2. Clairon 4
3. Trompette 8
4. Basson 16
5. Voix Humaine 8
6. Hautbois 8
7. Cymbale III
8. Plein Jeu IV-V
9. Doublette 2
10. Flûte Octaviente 4
11. Prestant 4
12. Voix Céleste T.C. 8
13. Gambe 8
14. Flûte 8
15. Diapason 8
16. Contre Viole 16
17. Octave
18. Bombarde to Swell

CHOIR (SWELL)
19. Corno di Bassetto 8
20. Double Trumpet 16
21. Mixture III
22. Wald Flute 2
23. Spitz Principal 4
24. Claribel Flute 8
25. Unda Maris T.C. 8
26. Salicional 8
27. Octave

CHOIR (GREAT)
28. Cornopean 8
29. Twentysecond 1
30. Nineteenth $1^{1}/_{3}$
31. Seventeenth $1^{3}/_{5}$
32. Fifteenth 2
33. Twelfth $2^{2}/_{3}$
34. Octave Flute 4
35. Geigen Principal 4
36. Flute 8
37. Open Diapason 8
38. Contra Dulciana 16

CHAIRE
39. Cremona 8
40. Ciderne III
41. Tierce $1^{3}/_{5}$
42. Recorder 2
43. Nasard $2^{2}/_{3}$
44. Rohrflöte 4
45. Spitzflöte 4
46. Stopped Flute 8
47. Italian Principale 8
48. Bombarde to Choir/Chaire
49. Swell to Choir/Chaire
50. Bombarde to Pedal
51. Swell to Pedal
52. Great to Pedal
53. Choir to Pedal
54. Great and Pedal Combinations Coupled
55. Pedal to Choir Pistons

RIGHT JAMB

BOMBARDE
56. Tremulant
57. Tuba en Chamade 8
58. Clarin 4
59. Trumpet 8
60. Bombarde 16
61. Mounted Cornet V
62. Flageolet $1^{1}/_{3}$
63. Tertia $1^{3}/_{5}$

CHOIR PEDAL
89. Octave Flute 4
90. Flute 8
91. Bourdon 16

GREAT
92. Clarin 4
93. Trumpet 8
94. Bombarde 16
95. Reeds on Bombarde

64. Lieblich Piccolo	2		96. Fourniture IV-V		
65. Quint Flöte	$2^{2}/3$		97. Sesquialtera II		
66. Lieblich Flöte	4		98. Cor de Nuit	2	
67. Lieblich Gedeckt	8		99. Super Octave	2	
68. Lieblich Bordun	16		100. Quint	$2^{2}/3$	
69. Bombarde to Great			101. Grosse Tierce	$3^{1}/5$	
70. Swell to Great			102. Flûte Harmonique	4	
71. Choir to Great			103. Gemshorn	4	

PEDAL

			104. Octave	4
72. Tuba	4		105. Hohlflöte	8
73. Posaune	8		106. Stopped Diapason	8
74. Bombarde	16		107. Viola da Gamba	8
75. Ophicleide	16		108. Principal	8
76. Bombardon	32		109. Bourdon	16
77. Mixture IV			110. Principal	16
78. Choral Bass	4		111. Subbass T.C.	32
79. Octave Quint	$5^{1}/3$			
80. Bass Flute	8			
81. Holz Principal	8			
82. Octave	8			
83. Quint	$10^{2}/3$			
84. Subbass	16			
85. Violon	16			
86. Principal Bass	16			
87. Major Bass	16			
88. Double Open Bass	32			

ACCESSORIES

Eight adjustable manual pistons to Bombarde, Swell, Great; Ten to Choir (5+5); Eight adjustable Pedal pistons; Reversible pistons to Great to Pedal, Swell to Great, Choir/Chaire to Great; Reversible pedal pistons to Great to Pedal, Swell to Great, 16ft Ophicleide; Full Organ toe piston; Illuminated switch Choir (Gt.) on Great; Thumb piston Doubles off; Six General pistons; general cancel piston.

NAVE CONSOLE (3 manual; drawstops)
    LEFT JAMB

SWELL			CHAIRE		
1. Tremulant			39. Cremona	8	
2. Clairon	4		40. Ciderne III		
3. Trompette	8		41. Tierce	$1^{3}/5$	
4. Basson	16		42. Recorder	2	
6. Hautbois	8		43. Nasard	$2^{2}/3$	
8. Plein Jeu IV-V			45. Spitzflöte	4	
9. Doublette	2		46. Stopped Flute	8	
11. Presant	4		47. Italian Principal	8	

12. Voix Céleste T.C.	8		49. Swell to Chaire	
13. Gambe	8		54. Great to Pedal	
14. Flûte	8		Combinations Coupled	
51. Swell to Pedal				
52. Great to Pedal				
53. Chaire to Pedal				

RIGHT JAMB

PEDAL			GREAT	
74. Bombarde	16		93. Trumpet	8
77. Mixture IV			61. Mounted Cornet V	
81. Holz Principal	8		96. Fourniture IV-V	
83. Quint	$10^{2}/3$		99. Super Octave	2
84. Subbass	16		100. Quint	$2\,^2/3$
85. Violon	16		101. Grosse Tierce	$3^1/5$
87. Major Bass	16		102. Flûte Harmonique	4
BOMBARDE (on Chaire)			104. Octave	4
62. Flageolet	$1^1/3$		106. Stopped Diapason	8
64. Lieblich Piccolo	2		108. Principal	8
66. Lieblich Flöte	4		109. Bourdon	16
67. Lieblich Gedeckt	8			
56. Tremulant			70. Swell to Great	
57. Tuba en Chamade			71. Chaire to Great	
(by piston)	8			

ACCESSORIES

Four adjustable manual pistons to Swell, Great, Chaire; Four adjustable Pedal pistons; Toe piston to Great to Pedal; Thumb pistons Great to Pedal, Swell to Pedal; Mobile platform, 60 feet of cabling.

Smaller organs in the Cathedral are the Choir Organ and St. George's Chapel Organ.

St. Andrew's Parish Church, Newgate Street, Newcastle upon Tyne

Running alongside his post as sub-Organist at the Cathedral, Clifford had an appointment as Organist and Choirmaster of St. Andrew's, probably in 1938 until some time before he was called for war service.

Although serving the church for a relatively short period he soon became greatly valued. An extract from the Church Magazine for April, 1939, reads:

> 'There have been few changes in any direction and the only recruit to our official staff is our organist and choirmaster, Mr. Clifford Harker, FRCO, in place of Mr. Harold Oswald who passed away at this time twelve months ago, and whose memory will be ever present with us. Mr. Harker is a worthy and most able successor. We are indeed fortunate. He has without the slightest difficulty and without causing any jerk to anybody, taken over the directorship of our

music. Having regard to the long and notable service of his predecessor this is a fine achievement for so young a man. We were well aware of his outstanding musical gifts before he came, sound judgement and great consideration for others - geniuses are not always sensible or pleasant fellows!

The attendance at the Three Hours Service was good and Good Friday evening particularly so. The Passion music we thought was more appreciated than ever this time and certainly beautifully rendered.'

All Saints Cathedral, Cairo

Brief details of Cairo's Anglican Cathedral will, no doubt, prove interesting historical reading, considering its particular importance during the Second World War, and Clifford's association for four years during that war.

Arthur Burrell's book 'Cathedral on the Nile' describes the whole story, and the remainder of this section deals mainly with the period of the War from his viewpoint. The full account, however, makes graphic and dramatic reading, covering the founding of the Cathedral up to 1984, when his book was written.

Cairo, the capital of Egypt, had existed from the earliest days. It was the Babylon of the Greeks and Romans, and of the ancient Hebrews, for it was the place to which the Jewish King and many leading citizens were taken into exile in 597 BC. A Jewish synagogue existed in Old Cairo, its origins no doubt dating to Old Testament times, but Christianity was brought to Alexandria by St. Mark, who is the accepted founder of the Church in Egypt.

The Anglican Church had its beginnings in the 19th century, when overland travellers to India passed through Cairo. The Church Missionary Society worked there and for a long time good relations existed between the two countries, with a gradual growing in number of British residents.

Fund raising for a cathedral was started in 1873 (four years after the opening of the Suez Canal) and the building, dedicated to All Saints, was ready by 1876. The Cathedral was to become a vital part of the life of the Anglican Church in Egypt in times of both peace and war.

Bishop Llewellyn Gwynne was given charge of the newly created diocese of Egypt and the Sudan in 1920, having previously been Assistant Bishop of Khartoum.

The building of a new Cathedral was started in 1936 and in 1938 the Cathedral on the banks of the Nile, designed by Gilbert Scott, was a place of beauty and elegance. 'The architect had achieved an impressive blend of both eastern and western features, which he had expressed in a harmonious unity.'

Archdeacon Frank Johnston arrived in 1933, and was to become Bishop of Egypt himself in 1952.

Arthur Burrell had been appointed Bishop's Chaplain just before war broke out in 1939, and his journey to Cairo was nothing short of an adventure; finding the Mediterranean route closed due to impending hostilities, he was obliged to travel overland to Venice and board an Italian boat, with its anti-British crew, arriving in Cairo towards the end of that year. His first Christmas there was, for him, unforgettable. He records in his book:

'The Cathedral attracted hundreds of worshippers. Obviously, there was something nostalgic about the services, and they also gave strength to face the uncertainties of the time. Five months later, a similar collection of worshippers was there. This time those present were far more aware of what was likely to be expected of them. The Allies had suffered enormous setbacks.

At the end of the second week of May, the German combined army and air force had broken through the Low Countries, violating their neutrality, Holland and Belgium were overrun......

The realities of the situation was all too obvious for the community in Egypt.'

Bishop Gwynne, in his 77th year, unconsciously assumed the role of spiritual leadership throughout the war. He issued instruction to all chaplains and missionaries at the height of the crisis "Stay at your posts whatever happens. Even if the worst happens, we shall be glad to have done so."

One familiar character in the British community was **Colonel Owen Pasha**. In his retirement from the Egyptian Army and Governorship of Luxor in World War I, one of his pursuits had been to write letters to the press about Hitler and his detestable enormities. With the threat of invasion of Egypt he was offered a guarantee of safe departure but, despite reprisals, he declared (among other forcible statements) that "The Bishop and Burrell are staying and, therefore, I should like to stay, too." Such was the courage inspired by the spirit of the Bishop. The Bishop's sermons put world events into perspective and inspired those present to get on with what they had to do - they were there to worship the Most High, to offer all they had and all they were in His service ...... that the malignant forces of evil should not prevail on earth.

After meeting Bishop Gwynne, a soldier wrote home "The Cathedral was HOME to many in khaki. Tea was served to anyone who went on Sunday afternoons in the Hall nearby, whilst evening services were packed completely with officers and men sitting all the way down the aisle with many standing elsewhere. If ever there was a sheet anchor or safe base it was the sureness of the Cathedral to lonely tommies or spiritually starved folk."

The music of the Cathedral had been in the hands of Gerhard Willner, an Austrian who, with his wife, had suffered grievously as Jews for their loyalty to their religion and race, and had been driven from Vienna by the Nazi regime. They were brilliant musicians and for four years served the Cathedral well, but took refuge in South Africa when Rommel's army threatened to advance. The 8th Army had already withdrawn to El Alamein, within 70 miles of Cairo.

Clifford's arrival seemed almost providential, and his work there has been recorded in Chapter 2.

The Cathedral was a haven during the whole of the war, with its Sunday worship and opportunities for people to attend lectures and study groups, all attempting to provide a diversion from the anxious situation.

A letter, published anonymously by the Ministry of Information in London, contained the words "Over it all, there is a feeling of genuine wholesome religion. It is all alive, all true, all wonderful. The Bishop catches them and holds them."

The 8th Army came under the command of General Montgomery in August, 1942, when Egypt had become threatened with invasion and, mercifully, by 1943 hostilities ceased in North Africa after the German Commander surrendered at Tunis. Although there was a more optimistic outlook there were still hundreds of service people moving through Cairo, on and up, gaining first Italy and, eventually, the whole European mainland. Many hundreds continued to experience and appreciate the positive encouragement of the Cathedral influence.

When hostilities ceased in Europe in 1945, victory was celebrated by the community in Cairo with great thankfulness, but many were conscious of a brittle and uneasy peace which brought difficulties almost as great as those experienced in war. For some years there had been smoulderings of revolutionary change which eventually fanned to vicious fire and brought about the end of Egyptian monarchy. It also engendered growing anti-British feelings and the Cathedral and community there came under increasing threat, with some ugly incidents.

Clifford remained in the Middle East until the Autumn of 1945 and, fortunately, was not there to become affected by the tensions as they developed in Anglo-Egyptian relations. The Cathedral continued to play a valuable role in ministering to a number of British residents in Cairo, although British troops were moved to the Canal Zone. Britain was nearing the tail-end of her influence in the country.

In 1951, Field Marshal Montgomery unveiled the 8th Army Memorial Window in the Cathedral - a grand occasion for the Cathedral community - but the next few months witnessed a serious decline in friendly relations between the British and Egyptian Governments, and violent clashes in the Canal Zone eventually brought about an abrogation of the Anglo-Egyptian Treaty. Fanatical mobs destroyed much of what had formed the centre of British social life. Relations between the British and Egyptians waxed and waned over the next twenty-odd years, but the Cathedral's witness remained firm; it adapted to a new situation and the Christian community began to hold services in Arabic in addition to English. Following a period of transition, the entire staff came to consist of Egyptian clergy, and so the Christian community of Egypt took on the responsibilities of the Church, under the leadership of devout ordained clergy, giving heart to all concerned, and although the Cathedral of 1938 was eventually replaced by a new building, the Christian body in Cairo grew steadily in worship and witness.

30. Cairo Cathedral exterior, 1942.
31. Cairo Cathedral interior.
32. The organ of Cairo Cathedral.

Relations between Britain and Egypt continued to deteriorate, resulting in the Suez Canal confrontation in 1956, but shortly before this there was anxiety over the site on which the Cathedral stood. It had been built on the site of a disused lock, running from the old Ismailian Canal, and flood waters seeped under the foundations, causing uneven settlement. During the political crisis no permanent repairs could be made and it became more and more expedient that another site be sought where a new building could be erected. What was also apparent was the fact that, for years, the increasing tide of traffic in Cairo was making the Cathedral almost an island, being surrounded by an almost constant flow of every kind of vehicle and noise, for a wide road was being prepared approaching the new Rameses Bridge, which was being built over the Nile. All buildings obstructing the road building were to be demolished, and so plans were made for an alternative site for a new building.

In 1974, a 'son of Egypt' was enthroned as Bishop, to lead the people forward, and the new Cathedral was consecrated in 1976.

Of the **Cathedral organ**, so capably played by Clifford for four years, not much is known, although it was almost certainly a quality instrument which served the Cathedral well, despite the dry Egyptian climate. During the building of the new Cathedral, Arthur Burrell noted in his book that the organ was removed from the old All Saints and placed temporarily in the new Assembly Hall by Messrs. Rushworth and Draper (at the expense of the Diocesan Association in Britain) until it could be built into its new setting.

St. Andrew's, Rugby

The opportunity for Clifford to become associated with St. Andrew's Church, Rugby in 1945, arose due to the death of Mr. Edward Groocock, who had been organist there since 1918.

The original church had been there for several centuries but by the mid-nineteenth century the fabric of the building became increasingly unsafe and a project for a completely new and bigger building was set in motion. The consecration took place in October, 1879, but it was not until 1896 that the tower, spire, and vestry were dedicated. The tower and spire stood magnificently at 182 feet high, and a peel of eight bells were placed in the tower.

Canon Henry Wolfe Baines was the incumbent when Clifford arrived. He was a lover of music and records show that 'with the co-operation of Mr. Clifford Harker as Organist and Choir-master, he raised the music of the church to a high level and the whole character of the services to great reverence, dignity and beauty'.

The organ had a long history. Originally, it was a small instrument with nineteen stops built, according to one record, by Father Bernard Schmidt who flourished from 1680 to 1706, whilst another record attributes it to Ralph Dallans, who died in 1672. It had been in the church of Norton-by-Galby, Leicestershire. In 1792 it was offered for sale and was purchased by Rugby

33. St. Andrew's Church, Rugby.

Parish Church by subscription, the sum collected being £395.2s.3d.

For a long time it stood in the western gallery of the old church. In 1841 the organ was rebuilt and enlarged by Nicholson of Worcester, a wing being added on either side of the old case, and the scale transferred from G to C.

After the rebuilding of the church the organ was reconstructed by Bishop and Son, of London, at a cost of about £900, and was placed in the south transept. It then contained 32 speaking stops, but the result was not altogether satisfactory and further alterations were made in 1892, and again in 1905, by Foster and Andrews of Hull. This firm overhauled and enlarged the instrument in 1915 and further additions were made in 1926, the speaking stops being increased to a total of 43. The number of pipes was then reckoned at 2,615, the front pipes being decorated in silver with gilt mouths and tops. In 1948, a standard pedal board was inserted. Further overhauls and additions were made and by 1963 it was considered that the instrument was one of the finest in the Midlands.

Cathedral Church of the Holy and Undivided Trinity, Bristol

When Clifford first arrived in Bristol he was more than impressed by the grandeur of the interior design of the nineteenth century hall-church, the Nave and the Aisles rising to the full height of the building, thus creating an impression of immense height and giving full view of the whole ceiling even to the furthest end of the Nave and through to the magnificence of the Lady Chapel at the eastern end, with its uniquely designed window.

He had been told that the windows in Bristol Cathedral, particularly beautiful with some dating back to the original church, had been removed to a safe place during the was years, being replaced by plain glass for the duration. There were 77 air raids on Bristol and when a thousand-pound bomb dropped in the road outside the Cathedral the windows were blasted out along that side of the building. It was during the Bristol blitz that a faithful band of 'Fire Watchers' braved an exposed position on the Cathedral roof, quickly and skilfully catching incendiary bombs that fell on to the roof, and tossing them by their fin on to the ground below. Thus, serious damage to the Cathedral was avoided. Clifford noticed the special window placed in the Nave to honour these incredibly brave people.

He soon learned to love the Walker organ, using its vast range to the full, and never tiring of being at the console playing, or giving instruction to his attentive organ students.

Clifford was the 29th organist since the Abbey of St. Augustine became the Cathedral Church in 1542.

The details and specification of this organ are reprinted from Clifford's own booklet 'The Organs in Bristol Cathedral' which he produced in 1952 (reprinted in 1976).

'In 1682 the Dean and Chapter gave orders to Renatus Harris, one of the foremost organ builders of the seventeenth century, for the erection of a

34. Bristol Cathedral – rear and garden.
35. Bristol Cathedral – Nave.

"fair great organ". This organ, which was placed in the screen, was completed in 1685, the year in which Bach and Handel were born. The two bays, as seen today, were originally the west and east fronts of the screen organ; the front pipes also date from 1685. The case (of which the western bay in particular is a magnificent example of seventeenth-century carving) was somewhat mutilated when it was moved from the screen.

'Renatus Harris's organ had three manuals, Great, Echo (the forerunner of the Swell) and Choir. The Choir had no individual pipes but some of the Great stops were "borrowed by communication". It was not until 1786 that a separate Choir organ of five stops was added by Seede, the pipes being placed behind the organ seat. Later still, in 1821, an octave and a half of pedals were added to operate the lower keys of the Great organ; there were no pedal pipes. Further additions were made in 1838, and then in 1860, when many alterations were made to the interior of the Cathedral, the organ was rebuilt and enlarged by W. G. Vowles, and moved from the screen to the north side of the Choir. "Equal temperament" tuning was adopted in 1867.

'The present organ dates from 1907, and was built by J. W. Walker and Sons, who incorporated the best of the previous organs. The work was carried out under the direction of Dr. H. W. Hunt, and with the generous financial help of Mr. H. O. Wills and other benefactors. The main improvements were the alteration of the compass of the manuals, the addition of the Solo organ, and the installation of tubular-pneumatic action. Original features preserved were the best of the old stops and, as mentioned above, the 1685 case-work and front pipes. Some further alterations and additions were made between 1947 and 1970.'

Specification of the present Walker Organ

GREAT		SWELL	
Double Open Diapason	16	Bourdon	16
Open Diapason (large)	8	Horn Diapason	8
*Open Diapason (medium)	8	†Open Diapason	8
*Open Diapason (small)	8	†Stopped Diapason	8
†Stopped Diapason	8	Dulciana	8
Wald Flöte	8	Vox Angelica	8
Principal (large)	4	†Principal	4
*Principal (small)	4	†Harmonic Flute	4
Flute	4	†Twelfth	2²/3
†Twelfth	2²/3	†Fifteenth	2
†Fifteenth	2	Sifflet	1
†Mixture	3 rks	†Mixture	3 rks
Double Trumpet	16	Contra Fagotto	16
Trumpet	8	Horn	8
Clarion	4	Oboe	8
		†Clarion	4
		Tremulant	

36. Bristol Cathedral - organ case and choir.
37. The Eastern Lady Chapel Choir Organ, Bristol Cathedral.

CHOIR		SOLO	
Double Dulciana	16	Harmonic Flute (unenclosed)	8
Open Diapason	8	Gamba	8
†Stopped Diapason	8	Voix Celeste T.C.	8
Viol di Gamba	8	Harmonic Flute	4
Dulciana	8	Cor Anglais	16
†Flute	4	Clarinet	8
Gemshorn	4	Orchestral Oboe	8
Fifteenth	2	Tromba (unenclosed)	8
Sesquialtera	2 rks	Tremulant	

PEDAL		COUPLERS
Double Open Diapason	32	Great to Pedal
†Open Diapason (wood)	16	Swell to Pedal
Open Diapason (metal)	16	Choir to Pedal
Violone	16	Solo to Pedal
Contra Gamba	16	Swell to Great
†Bourdon	16	Choir to Great
Dulciana	16	Solo to Great
†Principal	8	Swell to Choir
Stopped Diapason	8	Swell super-octave
Octave Quint	$5^{1}/3$	Swell sub-octave
Flute	4	Swell unison off
Trombone	16	Great pistons to Pedal combinations
Trumpet	8	Pedal basses to Swell pistons

*Renatus Harris, treble revoiced   †Old, but later partly revoiced

Thumb pistons: Great 5, Swell 5, Choir 3, Solo 5
5 pedal pistons duplicating Swell thumb pistons, and 5 pedal pistons controlling Pedal organ stops
2 double-acting thumb pistons and pedal pistons controlling Swell to Great and Great to Pedal.
1 pedal piston to draw Pedal reeds.
Balanced swell pedals to Swell and Solo organs.
There are 3,461 pipes in the organ; the smallest is a quarter of an inch in length, and the largest thirty-two feet.

The Lady Chapel Organ

The organ in the Eastern Lady Chapel, built by Harrison and Harrison, was presented to the Cathedral by Mr. H. P. Chadwyck-Healey in 1956. The organ case, designed by Mr. R. H. Brentnall, incorporates the surviving parts of the 1786 Choir organ. The five stops are: Stopped Diapason 8, Flute 4, Principal 4, Fifteenth 2, Mixture 2 ranks.

St. Mark's, the Lord Mayor's Chapel, Bristol

One unusual fact about this building is that it is not a parish church. It is the only building that remains of the Mediaeval Hospital founded about

38. C.H. at the organ of Bristol Cathedral.

1220 by Maurice de Gaunt, grandson of Robert Fitzharding, founded of the Abbey of St. Augustine in 1140 (now the Cathedral).

Henry VIII sold it to the Mayor of Bristol and it was granted to the French Protestant (Huguenot) refugees in 1687. It became the official place of worship for the Mayor and Corporation in 1721. Bristol is the only city in England which has a chapel as the exclusive property of the commonalty.

The first **school** to be established in the buildings of the dissolved Hospital of the Gaunts was **Queen Elizabeth's Hospital** and when this school moved to new buildings in about 1732, the **Bristol Grammar School** occupied the buildings until 1877.

Since 1722, the chapel has been the official place of worship for the Corporation and it is still maintained by the City and County of Bristol.

In 1889 the building was thoroughly restored, retaining some interesting features, and the nineteenth century choir stalls have attractive misericords. The small chapel has sixty-four pew seats which provide seating for the number of City Councillors at that time, whilst there are also seats reserved for the officers of the Council, and larger ones for the Lord Mayor and Lord Lieutenant or Lord Mayor's Consort. Also built in 1889 was a cloister for use as a choir vestry.

W.G.Vowles built the organ in the 1880s. The console was moved from the south to the north side in the 1960s during rebuilding by Percy Daniel and Co. Ltd., of Clevedon. Revisions were again carried out by Percy Daniels in 1978 under a scheme drawn up in consultation with the then Director of Music, Dr. Nigel Davison.

Organ Specification

Detached drawstop console of two manuals.

GREAT		PEDAL	
1. Double Open Diapason	16	1. Open Wood	16
2. Open Diapason	8	2. Open Diapason	16
3. Wald Flute	8	3. Bourdon	16
4. Dulciana	8	4. Lieblich Bourdon	16
5. Principal	4	5. Principal	8
6. Flute	4	6. Bass Flute	8
7. Twelfth	$2^{2}/3$	7. Octave Quint	$5^{1}/3$
8. Fifteenth	2	8. Octave Flute	4
9. Mixture 19.22	2 ranks	9. Mixture 19.22	2 ranks
10. Trumpet	8	10. Fagotto	16
SWELL		COUPLERS	
1. Lieblich Bourdon	16	Swell to Great	
2. Open Diapason	8	Swell to Pedal	
3. Stopped Diapason	8	Great to Pedal	
4. Salicional	8	Great to Pedal Combinations Coupled	

39. The Lord Mayor's Chapel, College Green, Bristol.

5. Voix Celeste T.C.	8		
6. Gemshorn	4	ACCESSORIES	
7. Flute	4	4 adjustable thumb pistons to Swell	
8. Fifteenth	2	4 adjustable thumb pistons to Great	
9. Sifflotte	1	4 toe pistons to Swell	
10. Mixture 22.26.29	3 ranks	4 toe pistons to Great	
11. Contra Fagotto	16	1 reverser Swell to Great	
Tremulant		1 reverser Great to Pedal	
Swell Octave			
Swell Suboctave			
Swell Unison Off			

Recitals

Clifford used his instruments with complete confidence and authority, whether he was playing a delicate *gigue* or grand fugue. His skills and manipulation sought out the finest possible tones.

He became known throughout the West Country as an organist of repute, gaining the respect of all who heard him.

Over the years he made a worthy contribution to the **Bristol and District Organists' Association**, becoming its President no less than three times - in 1952, 1962 and 1976, which is particularly noteworthy.

In his youth he had doubtless many opportunities to play for church services, when voluntaries would be needed, and his own style of extempore playing would have developed during the years before the war.

Working for his Associateship (1932), followed by a Fellowship of the Royal College of Organists in 1933, at the age of 21, would require a thorough knowledge of the organ and real expertise by the time Clifford was serving as organist in **Newcastle**.

In those **Cairo** years, there was regular playing for services and opportunities for organ recitals in addition to all the work in which he was involved through Music for All. Although there is no record of what music he played, some of his compositions for organ were published before the war and, undoubtedly, these would sometimes feature in his programmes.

Rugby, also, heard Clifford's organ skills as he was heard regularly in church services. His voluntaries included many classic favourites: Rheinberger: Cantilena; Mendelssohn: Finale from the 4th Sonata; Vierne: Carillon; Bach: Prelude and Fugue in B minor; Bonnet: Variations de concert. In Rugby recitals he was known to expound pieces like César Francke: Choral in B minor; Arne: A Fancy; Widor: Toccata in F.

When **Bristol** provided the great Walker organ, again his enthusiasm for the instrument showed tremendous virtuosity in his regular and popular recitals and he often concluded with a major organ work such as Bach's Passacaglia and Fugue in C minor, or a showy toccata.

David Jewell, in his appreciation of Clifford at a Farewell Dinner proclaimed "How well he played, and how those recitals were enjoyed. Over the whole period of Clifford's residence in Bristol he has given great pleasure and satisfaction with his organ recitals." In his own humorous manner, David remembered his own experiences with the instrument - it was a far cry from his early days when he had pumped the organ blower in a small Methodist chapel in West Cornwall. One day, after modernisation, with electrics, automatic couplings, and so on, the lady organist told him she could now change her combinations without moving her feet! David said (amidst much laughter) that he had tried, but he couldn't!

David Jewell remembered Clifford's recitals and the delightful music he played - Bach recitals, English music, Francke, and the French School - Vierne, Alain and Langlais. So many people would remember those recitals with great pleasure.

The **Lord Mayor's Chapel** organ ensured that Clifford did not lose his touch (or become out of touch). Retiring from the Cathedral meant that he had left a job he dearly loved and on meeting up with **Michael Doswell** in Newcastle shortly afterwards there was a feeling of sadness about him. But shortly after that visit Michael heard from him that a new opportunity had presented itself. "They've asked me to be organist at the Lord Mayor's Chapel. A nice job for my retirement, I think!" And so it was! It gave him the necessary stimulus to continue his lifelong love of music, the organ and service to the church. There were not many recitals during those years but he enjoyed arranging frequent recitals at the Chapel and his heart was full. He had enough strength and enthusiasm to continue to create a reverent atmosphere during services and to make a meaningful contribution in the gentler atmosphere of a more intimate sanctuary.

Over a fulfilling lifetime, Clifford Harker had played the organ in churches near and far. Invitations for recitals had not restricted him to playing in churches, however, as a student under Sir Malcolm Sargent, it is likely that he had only one experience of playing the organ in the Royal Albert Hall, but the organ of the Colston Hall, Bristol, felt his touch from time to time, as did the organ of the Great Hall of Bristol University.

Clifford was also glad to give recitals in smaller places, such as the Lord Mayor's Chapel (long before he became organist there), and the attractive church in Abbots Leigh, when he would tailor his programmes to compliment the smaller organ and give immense pleasure to local people.

When finally persuaded to make recordings, Clifford was happy to oblige and with Rex Hipple produced a worthy recording (a co-production between the City of Bristol Museum and Art Gallery and the Friends of Bristol Cathedral) featuring Clifford playing the fine Walker organ. Items played included: du Mage: Grand jeu; Flor Peters: Prelude on 'O God, thou faithful God'; Healey Willan: Processional; Louis Vierne: Berceuse; Clifford Harker: Prelude on 'Iste Confessor'; Bach: Two chorale preludes - 'Adorn Thyself, my soul' and 'Today God's Son triumphed' . . . . . an equal triumph for Clifford Harker!

This chapter does not claim to be in any way a complete and extensive record, but what is known has been set down as a guide to Clifford's expertise with the various organs at his disposal, and the places where he played, with some of his favourite music.

CHAPTER 6
COMPOSITIONS AND ARRANGEMENTS
'With wonderful deathless ditties'

This section relates to the music written or arranged by Clifford Harker, in addition to the listings in Chapter 2.

A complete catalogue would be impossible to compile, as much of his early musical writing does not now exist, some having been considered by Clifford himself 'youthful indiscretions' and not retained.

Having studied composition at the Royal College his early attempts would almost certainly have been tried out and the 1935 Scarborough programme (Chapter 2) is a good indication that he was confident of its quality and keen to have it played.

However, those of his published compositions that can be accounted for are listed, together with all known original pieces and arrangements. If some are catalogued only by title at least it indicates something of the spread of his capabilities.

The full extent of Clifford's writing will never be known but his musical interpretations of the Psalms were numerous. Unfortunately, although excellent, most have long gathered dust on library shelves. His anthems and Services were greatly appreciated at services, but his setting of George Herbert's 'Come my Way, my Truth, my Life' was a particular favourite; Dr. Ben Burrows is said to have been very thrilled with the piece and overwhelmed when it was dedicated to himself.

As a composer, Clifford was characteristically unassuming about his ability, always acknowledging his indebtedness to Vaughan Williams (whose first remark to him was that he had been unwise to leave the tutelage of Dr. Burrows, whom VW described as the finest teacher in the country, in order to learn to write "consecutive fifths and bad Bach" from himself). Clifford's modest response to compliments on his inventions would be "Oh, just a bit of bad Vaughan Williams, you know."

The early disciplines learnt from his father were partly responsible for Clifford's ability to write so well. He always said he could 'hear' the music as he was composing or arranging, and that must surely be a natural asset when scoring.

Many orchestral players commented on his good writing. He scored particularly well for timpani, as John Giddings was keen to point out - probably because it was his 'third instrument'! But he was most sensitive in his writing and his devotional and organ compositions were the best one could get in English church music, keeping in total harmony with the church surroundings.

His published organ pieces are played in many parts of the world and copies of his music are used as far away as New Zealand.

Clifford produced original music for the Guild of Cathedral Players' dramas which, if available now, could well prove to be some of the finest he wrote.

His carol arrangements became a legend to Bristolians and he sometimes arranged snippet orchestral parts when organising his concerts. One outstanding instance is Harker's arrangement of Elgar's National Anthem and, once, when performing the Verdi 'Requiem' in the Colston Hall, he arranged the parts for four trumpets and horns so that only two trumpets needed to go off to play as Distant Trumpets, whilst the other players remained in the orchestra. A cunning way of using his resources!

Anyone reading from Clifford's manuscripts would find it an interesting experience; probably better, though, than most other composers' originals, and certainly large enough to read!

But, then, his handwriting, too, was 'interesting', and has been described in various ways:

> 'an A4 page with twenty words in the infamous writing covering the whole page.'
>
> 'a script that looks as though it was produced by a wooden skewer.'
>
> 'written in his characteristic bold, outsize, handwriting.'

. . . .

Organ Music

1935	Two Idylls for Organ. Set 1.	Novello
1939	Three Preludes based on French Church Melodies	Novello

    1. Iste confessor (Rouen church melody)
    2. Iste confessor (Angers church melody)
    3. Solemnis haec festivas (Angers church melody)
    Dedication: To my Father.

1939	Solemnis haec festivas. Prelude on an Angers church melody (Selected Easter Pieces for Organ)	Novello
1957	Four Miniatures for Organ	Bosworth

    1. Elegy   2. Variations on a Genevan theme
    3. Simplicitas   4. Exsultate

1961	Pastoral Suite (Novello's Organ Music Club No. 23)	Novello

    1. Pastourelle   2. Musette   3. Scherzetto

1961	Three Easy Postludes for Organ 1, 2 (In memoriam), 3.	Bosworth
1964	Prelude on 'Westminster Abbey'	Bosworth
1976	Rouen Processional, based on the Rouen tune 'Coelites plandant' (The Cathedral Organist Series. Eight Works by various organists) **Dedicatio: John Jenkins**	Cramer

Undated

Concerto in D. Avison, arr. CH.	Novello
Three Pieces founded on Plainsong	Bosworth
Cantilena and Alla marcia (in a 2 stave volume)	Novello

40. First page of 'Iste Confessor'.

Anthems and Services
1939　Holy Father, cheer our way.　Evening anthem　　Novello
　　　(chorus and organ) (words by R.H. Robinson, 1842-92)
1956　O God of Bethel (Founded on the tune 'Strathcaro')　Novello
1958　Two Introits (SATB Unacc.)　　　　　　　　　Novello
　　　　　1. Bread of the World
　　　　　2. Come my Way, my Truth, my Life
　　　　Dedication: To Dr. Ben Burrows
1962　Te Deum in F. New Canterbury Series (chorus and organ)
　　　　　　　　　　　　　　　　Ascherberg, Hopwood & Crew
1963　O Lord God. The Collect for Sexagesima　　Novello
　　　　(SA(T)B and organ)
1963　Communion Service in G　　　　　　　　　　Novello
　　　　(chorus and organ)
1976　Laudate Dominum
　　　　(chorus, brass, timpani and organ)
　　　　(original manuscript copy in 1976 Diocesan Festival Book)

Undated
　　　Evening Service in D (Unison)　　　　　Novello
　　　Evening Service in A flat　　　　　　　OUP
　　　Thou O God art praised (Corfe arr. CH)　OUP
　　　Blessed is the man (Corfe arr.CH)　　　OUP
　　　At the Lamb's high feast　　　　　　　　OUP
　　　Psallite unigenito　　　　　　　　　　　Unpublished

Carol Arrangements
1956　Come, good folk (French trad.)　　　　　Novello
1962　*My Dancing Day. (Trad. carol)　　　　　Novello
　　　　(SATB unacc.)
1965　*I saw three ships (Trad.) (New Canterbury Series) Ascherberg
　　　　(Mixed voices. unacc.)
1969　*Away in a manger (Words W.J. Kirkpatrick)
　　　　(manuscript copy)
　　　* Dedication: For Bristol Cathedral Special Choir

Undated
Angels from the realms of glory (Trad.)
Angelus ad virginem (13th century English)
Awake and join (Dorset. arr. male voices)
Break forth, O beauteous heavenly light (Bach)
Deck the Hall (Welsh)
Ding dong merrily on high (Trad.)
Earth today rejoices (piae cantiones 1582)
Good King Wenceslas (piae cantiones)
King Jesus hath a garden (Dutch)
Love came down at Christmas (Tune: CH)
O little one sweet (17th cent.)

Of the Father's heart (16th cent. processional)
Rocking (Czech)
See amid the winter's snow (Goss)
Silent Night (Austrian)
Sleepers wake (Mendelssohn)
Sweet was the song (Tune from Wm. Ballett's Lute Book)
The Angel Gabriel
The Cradle
The holly and the ivy (Trad.)
The Maker of the sun and moon (Dorset)
The Noble Stem of Jesse (Praetorius, arr. for male voices)
The seven joys of Mary
The shepherd's cradle song (German, arr. for male voices)
The Son of God (Praetorius)
To us in Bethlem city (17th cent. arr. for male voices)

Carols orchestrated for Cathedral Carol Evenings
Deck the Hall (SATB and orchestra)
Good King Wenceslas (Boys, SATB and orchestra)
Hark, the glad sound
While shepherds watched
Nowell
Hark, the herald angels sing
The holly and the ivy
It came upon the midnight clear
Lo, star-led chieftains (Words Wm. Crotch)
The Manger Throne (Words C. Steggall)
O little town of Bethlehem
Of the Father's heart (Piae cantiones 1582) (SATB, orchestra & organ)
Once in Royal David's city (boys, SATB, orchestra, organ, congregation)
Rocking (Czech) (Boys (2-part) SATB, solo oboe & strings)
See amid the winter's snow (Goss) (SATB, Boys (unison) & orchestra)
Silent Night (Austrian) (Boys (2 part), SATB & orchestra)
The Son of God is born (14th cent.)

Original compositions

1935	Meditation (orchestrated)	unpublished?
1958	The owl and the pussy cat (SATB)	Elkin
	(A nonsense song by Edward Lear)	

Undated

A wet sheet and a flowing sea (unison)	Novello
I wandered lonely (unison)	Novello
Orpheus with his lute (unison)	Novello
The Sower's Song (2 part)	Novello
Two Elizabethan Songs (solo)	Novello

41. Part of manuscript arrangement by C.H. for distant trumpet (Verdi: Requiem).

CHAPTER 7
LEISURE ACTIVITIES - THE LIGHTER SIDE
*'O Man! It must ever be that we dwell, in our dreaming
and singing, a little apart from ye.'*

Clifford's life was very full - there was not a lot of time left after he had attended to all Cathedral duties, some teaching, and three choral rehearsals each week, but somehow short breaks were found to chat with friends - taking coffee or tea at one of his favourite restaurants, Brights (later Dingles) in Queen's Road, Clifton, and Horts or Carwardine's nearer the centre of the city.

Chorister parents provided good conversation and several friendships were formed which lasted throughout the years, although Clifford was always careful to guard his private life, and close friendships were rare. There was closer association with organ students and their families - John Jenkins and his parents, and the Dyer family - people who had close affinity with his interests. He sometimes visited John at the schools where he taught, taking a fatherly interest in John's work. He was once present at a school choir rehearsal and John asked Clifford to accompany the singing, which he did willingly. Afterwards he recounted his experience at the next Bristol Choral Society rehearsal as he knew members were always glad to have news of John, telling them how much he had enjoyed the experience and how, after the session, a boy had said to John "Please sir, who is the gentleman?" On being told a little about Clifford, the boy replied "He's awfully good, isn't he?" (little did he know!) Clifford's amused recounting of the incident brought forth a great laugh and round of applause.

Home was, for Clifford, for many years a small hotel room in Pembroke Road, Clifton, overlooking Buckingham Vale. Mr. and Mrs. Henry Palmer, the proprietors, did not see a lot of him but knew he spent a substantial amount of time there, working out his arrangements always to the loud accompaniment of ANY music coming from the radio. Their telephone was in frequent use and was of great value to him when working from home, or for people wishing to contact him.

Clifford enjoyed remarkably good health, and his thick, dark hair made up part of his character, not showing any sign of greying until he was well into his eighties. Because of this it was all too difficult to make any guess of his age, and he never divulged it.

There were one or two occasions when an accident or minor illness enforced an unplanned break but, even in these circumstances, he remained the perfect gentleman, accepting his temporary incapacity with customary dignity, always glad to receive visitors and being most appreciative of people's kindness and concern. Rex Hipple made more than one hospital visit to Clifford and his welcome was a timely reminder of the times when Clifford himself was known to make visits to hospital, particularly on

Christmas afternoon, returning to the Cathedral for said Evensong at 3.30 p.m.

Always the Elgarian, Clifford had a lively interest in the **Elgar Society**, founded in 1951, being critical to the success of the South West Branch in the early part of its formation. In 1978, Bristol members of the Elgar Society approached Clifford about the possibility of starting a branch in the area. After several discussions the proposal met with the approval of the main Society and the South West Branch came into being in 1979, with Clifford as its Chairman, supported by a properly elected committee. Clifford was also invited to become a Council member (of the main Society) which he accepted but found pressure of other duties too great to be able to travel to London for Council meetings on a regular basis. However, he remained Chairman of the South West Branch for three years and was always most supportive to the organisation. He showed a profound knowledge of Elgar's music and whenever an Elgar work was being performed by one of his choral societies he took groups of singers along to the Society meeting to give an illustrated talk about the work. Meetings were held in the Bristol Music Club in Clifton for a few years, moving to the Octagon at the Bristol Polytechnic, and then to Redland Church Rooms. He became Branch Patron in 1982 and remained in that office until his death. He was also elected an Honorary Member of the Elgar Society in 1994 - a rare distinction.

Life in Bristol involved frequent organ recitals - the Colston Hall, the Lord Mayor's Chapel, and Clifford received many invitations to play in churches both in Bristol and beyond. He also made many broadcast recitals.

Another adjunct of Clifford's musical absorption was his membership of the **Bristol and District Organists' Association**, of which he was to become three times its President - in 1953, in 1962 and in 1978.

The years of presidency were busy ones for Clifford. It was usual for the President to mastermind events for the year, being the figurehead for the Association. In one of Clifford's presidential years (1962), the National Congress of the Incorporated Association of Organists was held in Bristol, the National President that year being Francis Jackson, of York Minster. Clifford and his Committee made all the arrangements for those attending the Congress - booking hotel accommodation, arranging concerts and outings, generally making sure the weekend was an enjoyable and trouble-free affair.

The Bristol Association was founded in 1934, Presidents being elected for one year of office. It had a steady membership of around two hundred, all keen musicians who played to each other, gave organ recitals, and held regular outings to play organs in and around their own area, even further afield, and enjoying many other social events.

In recent years members of the Association became aware of the danger that a number of local organs might become redundant, and careful records were made of locations, historical data and, where possible, trying to find new 'homes' for such instruments to avoid their decay.

One very creditable action of the Bristol and District Organists' Association was to prevent the demise of the **Colston Hall organ**. In pre-war days there were frequent recitals on the fine concert organ made by Henry Willis & Sons, and the post of City Organist was usually held by a prominent local church organist. In 1945, after surviving the blitz of the war years, disaster struck in the form of a major fire which destroyed the Hall with its magnificent 'Father Willis'. Because of post-war restrictions the rebuilding of the Hall could not take place until 1950, when the new organ was built and installed by Harrison and Harrison of Durham. The post of resident organist was not reinstated and recitals were only occasional, although the instrument was often used at choral concerts. A period of neglect left the organ in need of costly repairs and moves were made to remove it altogether. This became the concern of the members of the Association and between 1995 and 2001 they spared no effort in encouraging more interest in the organ by arranging recitals throughout the year, often given by eminent musicians, thus financing the needful repairs and making the instrument once again highly valued and enjoyable to listen to. All this involved close liaison between the Association and the City Director of Entertainment, resulting in the magnificent organ being heard regularly once more. Such was the commendable enthusiasm of the Association members.

Whether just off-duty or on holiday, work was never far from his mind and Clifford never failed to make well-advanced preparation for future activities, in between short periods of happy relaxation - with music, of course - and with friends of like mind.

For holidays Clifford enjoyed a complete break in August by visiting his favourite resorts - Weston super Mare; Bournemouth and Sidmouth on the south coast; and, most often, Scarborough. This last resort was a particular favourite, especially as it held so many happy memories from his youth and he never tired of this place of pilgrimage. Even on holiday he liked style - in a wonderfully old-fashioned way, and he had his own inimitable style - one of quality and elegance. He loved to stay in what he called the 'posh' part of Scarborough, in a hotel on the front. He loathed anything cheap or second-rate, and thought the world was coming to an end when the Grand Hotel there was taken over by Butlins. He made sure he was in Scarborough for the cricket festival as he was a great supporter of Yorkshire Cricket Club.

He loved holidays abroad, too: Nice, Lucerne and the Austrian Alps, and some years visited countries of Scandinavia, enjoying the appeal of the cruise as much as the destination itself. In 1970 he had a Rhine holiday, visiting many interesting places in Germany. (His German was very good, displaying a Swiss accent). On arriving at Bonn Cathedral, Clifford grinned at his companions and said "Let's look at the music list and see if they're doing Stanford in C today."

Choir Tours

Overseas trips by the Choir of Bristol Cathedral started in the 1970s, and Clifford joined the party on two occasions, in 1981 and in 1983 (the year of his retirement).

Whenever a Choir Tour was planned many people became involved. Clifford was responsible for the music, naturally; he rehearsed the Choir and held himself responsible for copies and all details relating to recitals. **Horace Dammers** and his wife were instrumental in making most other arrangements, together with **Richard Chubb**, the Precentor, and his wife. One or two wives of the lay clerks and one or two chorister parents who made up the party helped with arrangements in some way or other. The whole choir went on tours and the expenses were subsidised, to some extent, by the Cathedral.

In **1981**, the Tour was first to **S. Benoit-sur-Loire**, then **Florence**, where they stayed for one week, followed by **Switzerland** and Notre Dame, **Paris**, on the return journey. It was an unforgettable experience for everyone in the party and invaluable experience for the choristers to have sung in different places and where the 'English tradition' was not the norm.

The pieces sung were taken from the Choir's normal repertory and Clifford arranged an interesting programme, with solo items by Stephen Foulkes (accompanied by Clifford) and, occasionally, organ pieces played by himself.

In Florence the Choir's efforts were greeted at the end with loud and prolonged cries of "Bravissimo, bravissimo". Then the Choir visited **Loppiano**, the headquarters of Focolare, a well-known international charismatic movement. Sitting in a large audience, they first had to listen to an Argentinian Rock band. Then (to quote Horace Dammers), "John Jenkins, Clifford's friend and Assistant, took his seat at an electronic keyboard more at home in Top of the Pops, and Clifford led the fully robed choir on to the podium. Grasping the microphone he announced "First the Choir will sing a piece from the sixteenth century." There followed pieces from the seventeenth, eighteenth and nineteenth centuries, stopping short of the twentieth but including, if I remember rightly, that sad but brave old favourite 'Never weather-beaten sail'. The Choir withdrew in favour of another pop group singing Christian lyrics, and the grand tradition of English cathedral music had been triumphantly maintained." Clifford was very glad to escape from the religious community but was almost despairing when a coach accident kept the party in Loppiano longer than anticipated.

In **Berne, Switzerland**, Clifford spoke in German to introduce items in a concert which received 'rave' reviews in the Swiss press, and on the way back to the ferry port the Choir was required to give a recital in a charming little church in a picturesque situation by a lake. The party members were billeted out to local people before and after the event and some hosts spoke excellent English (which was something of a relief to many of the Choir). The host and hostess of Stephen Foulkes attended the recital, and the Choir was resplendent in scarlet cassocks. Clifford walked on wearing his academic gown and, with a lift of his arms, the concert proceeded. Later, walking home with his host and hostess, Stephen remembered that the hostess had remarked how everybody in the audience had recognised the 'charisma' of the man as soon as he had walked on. She talked about an indefinable quality which very few people have. This compliment came from someone who had never seen Clifford before. Her impression was happily confirmed by her guest!

Clifford thoroughly enjoyed the tour, revelling in the beautiful churches visited.

And there was fun galore! One story was of an occasion when the lay clerks were dining in a restaurant in **Florence**, where the service was unbelievably slow. During an interminable wait for the meal to appear Clifford was induced into relating stories from his time in Cairo. Describing the RAF's dismal failure to train him in something technical he professed to have become the world's worst wireless operator, after which he said "They threw me out and put me into music." "And what were you like at that?" asked John Jenkins. Amid the general uproarious laughter thus caused, Clifford managed to say "O, very good." without batting an eyelid. Although this was spoken in jest it is further evidence that he was truly modest about his abilities. He was just not given to pretentiousness and the only pedestal he sought was a musical one. He knew intuitively what he was good at and did not pretend expertise in areas which he knew were not his forte.

The sequel to this incident was that, as the food in the restaurant was poor and very expensive, it tempted one of the party to react by picking up a small cushion on which he had been sitting, taking it away remarking that he felt entitled to it as compensation for the cost of a poor meal. He showed it to Clifford outside the restaurant who threw up his hands in mock horror. Then he said "Oh well, we'll keep it for the organ stool - it'll be a nice cushion for the organist's bum." Then he realised that one of the choristers' mums had heard him utter what he considered to be a rude word, and he immediately said "Oh, my dear lady, I'm so sorry, do forgive me!" Of course, no apology was needed and the chorister parent enjoyed the joke as much as anyone.

The Tour of **1983** was equally enjoyable, and delightful to audiences wherever the Choir sang. The visit was to **northern France**, in the spring, and was to be Clifford's final tour as he had already announced his intention to retire at the end of the Summer term, and the responsibilities of the project were likely to make many demands upon his physical stamina at the age of seventy-one.

However, it was a really happy tour, with concerts going well and everyone enjoying themselves. The Choir sang in two cathedrals, several churches, which included the **Church of St. Pierre at Caen**. The building had been completely destroyed during the war but had been restored to its former beauty.

Robert Weddle, Director of Music, who had previously been organist of Coventry Cathedral, and the people at St. Pierre, made the Choir most welcome as the visit had been anticipated with great pleasure. Robert Weddle sent his memories (on cassette) of the visit for Clifford's Retirement Dinner that year, and his words are reproduced here:

> 'The Tour had been extremely well planned. Several months before there had been an advance party to 'scout out the land'. Then, with perfect timing, the vanguard - a *de luxe* limousine - arrived five minutes before the main party in a coach. Out of the car 'uncoiled' Clifford, calm and unruffled, determined to be unhurried and determined to let other people do the rushing around, whilst he concentrated his own energy upon the music - good English church music, beautifully sung totally. The choir was Clifford's instrument, not only a choir trainer in the position of using his instrument, but building it. Over the years, that 'building' was quite unique, a sympathy, a homogeneity of sound. He didn't need to talk about 'style'; style had been forged over a period of many years. He was able to use his instrument not only with authority, but also with total honesty and simplicity.
> The audience was completely relaxed and, because they were relaxed, they enjoyed, and were very appreciative of the music. Clifford's own music had represented the best of what one had come to love in English church music, or music for the Anglican liturgy. Here was something which was very beautiful but not striving for effect, very controlled but beautifully poised as well. Friendships were made on both sides. It was a happy visit all round, and the only thing regretted was the last glimpse of Clifford coiling back into the car, the vanguard leading the way back to le Bec Helloin.'

Another stay was in **Orsay**, a religious community in the environs of Paris. **Stephen Foulkes** was in the party and relates an amusing incident which happened there:

> 'We each stayed in small but comfortable rooms prepared for visitors, but we were expected to obey the rules of the community which were posted at intervals along the walls of the corridors. These rules included 'Lights out at 10 o'clock', 'No Smoking', 'No drinking or eating in guest rooms' etc. Very inhibiting! A party of us, including Clifford, John (Jenkins) and several others, returned a little late to the hostel to find the main gates closed and locked. One of the younger lay-clerks climbed over the 8ft. wall to find another entrance. We wondered whether we should all have to climb the wall, and my wife, Gerry, said "Well, I'll climb it if I have to." Clifford said "Oh, will you, Gerry? In that case I will as well." The thought of our dignified and much loved organist sneaking over the wall was an image which still amuses today. Eventually, another door was found and we entered with relief. Gerry suggested that we

all return to our room to continue the party as it was our last night in Orsay, and everybody fell in with the plan. Soon our room was full of cigarette smoke and clinking bottles as we continued the party and somewhat chatted the night away. Clifford enjoyed his cigarettes, and joined in with good humour. He was always good fun to be with! Later, the party split up and returned as quietly as they could to their own rooms. Our litter bin was full of cigarette stubs and empty wine bottles! The couple in the next room to us later remarked that they had heard a bit of a noise during the night and wondered what had been going on. They assumed it was some of the younger lay-clerks having a party. We didn't mention that Clifford had been a participant!'

All who went on choir tours were to retain unforgettable memories, with their own special moments, but one thing that remained in their memory above all others was the puissant figurehead of Clifford Harker holding sway over the wonderful legacy of English Church Music.

. . . .

CHAPTER 8
IN RETIREMENT AND VALETE
'Yea, in spite of a dreamer who slumbers
and a singer who sings no more . . . . . .
we are the music makers.'

Days of semi-retirement were, for Clifford, very fruitful and his lifeline was most certainly the Lord Mayor's Chapel. He was able to take life at a more gentle pace and, whilst still enjoying the responsibilities of the post (and admirably fulfilling them), he was able to continue to live a full and purposeful life.

There were occasional recitals at the Chapel but he was quite happy for other musicians to provide interesting and enjoyable programmes at the Saturday afternoon recitals. He enjoyed introducing the performers and talking about the pieces to be played and, over the years, a great variety of music was given by the various soloists and instrumental ensembles, in addition to organ recitals.

As time went by, Clifford became less mobile and experienced difficulties with walking. Even so, he staunchly refused to use a walking stick or any kind of support, bravely endeavouring to retain his 'image'.

When he finally realised that the effort of retaining duties at the Chapel was getting too much, he quietly retired in 1996, after twelve years of faithful service.

Clifford became increasingly aware of the demise of physical activity and he was fortunate in obtaining accommodation in Worcester Court, very close to Vyvyan Terrace, where he had lived for a number of years. The flat was specifically geared for elderly people and had the advantage of a resident warden, should he need help at any time.

April, 1999, was another grand occasion for Clifford Harker. Her Majesty the Queen visited Bristol Cathedral for the Royal Maundy Service which was, naturally, accompanied by much pageantry. Amongst the people presented on that day was Clifford himself, who felt honoured to meet his Queen again at the place he loved so well.

He was then getting more immobile and it was necessary for him to have assistance into the Cathedral. This was by wheelchair, and on the way into the Cathedral he saw his good friend, **Alan Canterbury**, verger of the Lord Mayor's Chapel, who was also on his way there to help with stewarding duties. Clifford, conscious of his incapacity, gave Alan a cheery wave, putting him at his ease by saying "I'm not as bad as it looks, my boy." And so passed another memorable occasion in his favourite place.

From then on, Clifford lived quietly in his apartment, which had many conveniences for him and suited his physical needs. Friends visited regularly and he was kept up to date with people and places, and musical events going on in and around the city. News of the progress of former choristers was particularly welcome, and he was always glad to receive a visitor. His spirits were high and he enjoyed a joke and talks of old times with friends as they reminisced.

Clifford remained always impeccably dressed, and even in the last days of his life you could be sure he would be wearing either a sports jacket and flannels, collar and tie, or a dark blue suit, as though he were just about to depart to go and conduct Evensong.

It has been said by more than one person that Clifford was 'married to his music'. The fact that he never married and spent the larger part of his life without an immediate family meant that towards the end of his life it was a few intimate friends who supported and ultimately cared for this very private man. Solitude never troubled Clifford - he greatly valued friendships, but his whole life was driven by his complete absorption in musical activities and he was never happier than being engrossed in music or musical conversation.

He suffered a fall in his flat in the Autumn of 1999, which brought about the necessity of nursing care. He remained in Cote Nursing Home, just off the Downs in Bristol, for a few weeks but did not recover from the shock he received from the fall.

He died on All Souls' Day - 2nd November, 1999.

At the exact time of his death, the Cathedral Choir and Special Choir were rehearsing in the Cathedral, and the news was quickly relayed to them. Thus, within hours, congregation and Choir were prayerfully giving thanks for his life. When Malcolm Archer succeeded Clifford as organist he initiated what became a regular All Souls' Day Service, with a Requiem as its central feature. This service in 1999 included the glorious Requiem by Gabriel Fauré and was to have very special significance for those present.

When people began to assess the virtues of Clifford Harker's life, many sincere tributes were made. His had been an era of orderliness, dignity and elegance, and all these attributes were reflected in the way he lived. But many things had changed in his lifetime, and his was the example of one who had lived through those changes without, in the slightest, sacrificing his own conviction about essential principals. For most people he encompassed the cardinal virtues of justice, prudence, temperance and fortitude.

Several years earlier, **David Jewell** had caught the ethos of the man in a speech he made at a Retirement Dinner -

"There are some people who live by honesty and by fortitude; they are people who keep alive some hope of virtue - in short supply these days. They are easily recognised, these people, because they seem to have resources within themselves. In this sense they are free men. They recognise their dependencies upon others, but they are not slaves to fashion or flattery. They stand out in contrast to those who rely on resources outside themselves. Clifford Harker is such a man. He has great gifts as a musician, and has a joy in communicating the greatest of all arts, the universal language. For his love of God and his fellow man, for his rare combination of austerity and warmth, for his courage in adversity, and particularly his serenity in facing a serious illness at one time (triflingly referred to); for his gifts of friendship - he is admired by all."

John Jenkins - more brief, but with profound discernment:

"He was one of the best, one of the very best:
to pupils - one of the best examples
to performers - one of the finest directors
to audiences - one of the most inspired performers."

A funeral service worthy of the man was held on 15th November. His dear friend, John Jenkins, had ensured that no detail was forgotten and no task remained undone as he awaited the cortège in the brilliantly sunlit Cathedral.

The building filled to capacity and the funeral service proceeded. The sun shone exceedingly brightly through the high windows, generating an aura of celebration rather than mourning, and people were uplifted by the memory of this wonderful, fulfilled, and truly laudable life.

The sermon was preached by the **Very Reverend A. H. Dammers** who was Dean sometime during Clifford's residence at the Cathedral. He reflected upon Clifford's life there and his tremendous influence upon all with whom he was involved, relating his own personal illustration of why he felt he personally had cause to thank God for Clifford:

"During the Second World War, as organist at Cairo Cathedral, Clifford was well placed to organise a number of classical concerts in Cairo, Jerusalem and elsewhere, bringing much comfort and joy to hundreds if not thousands of service men and women, including myself. My brief, inglorious military career began in action at the battle of El Alamein in the Western Desert. During this battle I had an experience which led me to consider offering for training for ordination. Shortly afterwards while on sick leave in Cairo I visited the Anglican Cathedral to pray about this. This beautiful building, since demolished to make way for a new bridge over the Nile and approach road, was a fit background for such decision making prayer. This was enhanced by chance and providence, if you believe in providence, of the organist playing some quieter pieces of his Bach repertoire on the organ. What a wonderful setting for a decision that changed my life. I like to think reasonably enough that it was a younger Clifford up there on the organ stool.

In conclusion, I shall return briefly to the passage from Revelation that has just been read. If St. John the theologian's vision of the heavenly Jerusalem is anywhere near the mark, choral singing would appear to play a central part. Some of us will need a good deal of kindly and sensitive rehearsing if we are worthy to play our part. I have a fantasy, which of course you mustn't take too seriously, that it would be rather nice if Clifford were in charge of our particular section of the heavenly choir."

A special Choral Evensong, in thanksgiving for the life of Clifford Harker was held at the Cathedral on 29th January, 2000. This occasion was special in many ways, being the last chance for people to pay personal tributes and to give thanks for his life. Much preparation had been made and there was a chance for anyone who had particular desire to do so, to join in the augmented choir for that occasion. It was a privilege and joy to several hundred people to share in this last act of thanksgiving, and the music chosen was in the style he would have truly endorsed.

Following a morning choral rehearsal and a further rehearsal with the Cathedral Choir in the early afternoon, the Memorial Evensong took place, with all honour and esteem due to such a great person. Everyone wanted to be at their very best for Clifford, whose ashes occupied a special place on the high altar for the whole service.

Clifford's own music opened the service - the Introit 'Come, my Way, my Truth, my Life', followed by a favourite congregational Newman hymn 'Praise to the holiest in the height', which seemed to permeate an almost ethereal 'Gerontius' atmosphere that remained throughout the service. The whole ethos was as if Clifford were the driving force.

The Order of Evensong included all that he would have relished:
Psalm 138 : I will give thanks unto Thee, O Lord, with my whole heart. (tune: Harker)
Psalm 150 : O praise God in His holiness (tune: Stanford)
Lesson : Isaiah 40: 1-5
Hymn : Angel voices ever singing
Magnificat and Nunc Dimittis : Stanford in C
Lesson : Matthew 26: 6-13
Anthem : Elgar - Give unto the Lord
Hymn : Glorious things of Thee are spoken
Appreciations of Clifford Harker
Hymn : Now thank we all our God
Choir : Elgar - The Angel's farewell (The Dream of Gerontius)
  The choir was conducted by **Mark Lee**, Cathedral Organist, organ played by **David Hobourn**, Assistant Organist.
  David Johnston, a regular soloist for Clifford, renowned for his portrayal of Gerontius, sang the part with special perception, and **Pamela Rudge** sang the role of the Angel with beauty and much sympathy.

The Appreciations were given by two of Clifford's best friends and sincere admirers. The sentiments of **David Jewell** have already been recorded earlier in this chapter and in other parts of this volume, as have those of **John Jenkins**, but these further words are recorded for their aptitude and utmost sincerity:

John Jenkins: (referring to the woman at Bethany, who created her memorial in anointing the feet of Jesus) ". . . . so is Clifford remembered for the beautiful thing he did for God in enriching the worship of this place with music. Each of us would have our own impressions and memories of his unique character. Perhaps the most important quality is the one expressed most simply. He was genuine in all he said and did. He was honest, he was utterly dependable and he had great integrity. He was a real Christian, a real musician and a real gentleman, and for that we loved and respected him. I can find no greater tribute to any human being than to acknowledge the life-forming and inspirational influence that Clifford had upon so many of us; the extraordinary richness of music and love of beauty he gave us, and the supreme example he set which enabled us to become, I believe, better people.

"It is a privilege to have known him and learned from him, and a joy to be giving thanks for his life and his work in this glorious service here today, here in his beloved Cathedral. Clifford was very reticent about his singing voice, so he may not actually be singing with the angels, but I am sure that he will have already formed a very Special Choir of them. David Johnston referred to Clifford's interpretation of 'Gerontius' as having an 'extra dimension'. At the end of the service, as we listen to Elgar's sublime music, the extra dimension will doubtless be a resounding in heaven of Clifford's own musical spirit. May his good and faithful soul rest in peace and be risen in great glory for evermore."

A letter was written on November 1st, 1999, on the day before Clifford died, and which he never received, from **Martin Steel**, a former organ pupil and member of the Special Choir. "I owe so much to you, Clifford. You inspired me as a youngster and enabled me to reach beyond myself. I will never be able to thank you enough for all you gave me. You enabled me to become the person I am today."

Countless similar tributes were paid to Clifford, spontaneous and unanimous, many of his former choristers all asserting that they would not be following fine musical careers had it not been for his inspiration and example as a musician and as a Christian gentleman. From Michael Doswell, Clifford's first organ Assistant in 1949, right up to choristers who began with him towards the end of his career, all had inherited a standard, a benchmark, of how to understand, interpret, and communicate the music which he taught them to love - what Lionel Pike, in his Preface to one of his books, termed 'the incomparable training under a devoted cathedral organist'.

Following the very special and memorable Choral Evensong, a small party of close friends passed into the Cathedral gardens, a peaceful place, beautifully kept, where birds sing. There Clifford was laid to rest in a spot
St. Mark's, the Lord Mayor's Chapel, Bristol
One unusual fact about this building is that it is not a parish church.
It is the only building that remains of the Mediaeval Hospital founded about 1220 by Maurice de Gaunt, grandson of Robert Fitzharding,

42. The Cathedral Garden, Bristol, showing the headstone of Walford Davies, 1869-1941.

close to two other musicians whom he greatly admired - Hubert Hunt and Henry Walford Davies.

A choir bench was dedicated to him, together with other permanent memorials, and the Friends of Bristol Cathedral made the gift of a handsome Yamaha grand piano to the Cathedral, a cogent expression of their appreciation of Clifford and his work.

In November, 2000, the Bristol Choral Society gave a performance of 'The Dream of Gerontius', which was dedicated to his memory.

Clifford Harker's name will be remembered, and his influence felt, for many years to come, his memory lingering, like the fragrant flowers in the garden where he rests. The trumpets have sounded 'on the other side' for him; he has heard the Voice of Welcome "Well done, thou good and faithful servant."

But Clifford shall have the final word. In a speech at his retirement, he remarked: "Since coming to Bristol I've listened to an enormous number of sermons, so I'm going to end with a text. When I came to Bristol I read up all I could about the Abbey, and so on, and I came across a saying, or a piece of advice, given by Saint Augustine, and I've tried in a modest way to live up to this. He said
"**Pray** as though everything depends upon **God**,
and **work** as though everything depends upon **yourself**."

Clifford Harker

VALETE

Pereunt et imputantur - They pass away and an account is required. (Words on a sundial on the Norman buttress of the transept South of the tower in Bristol Cathedral.)

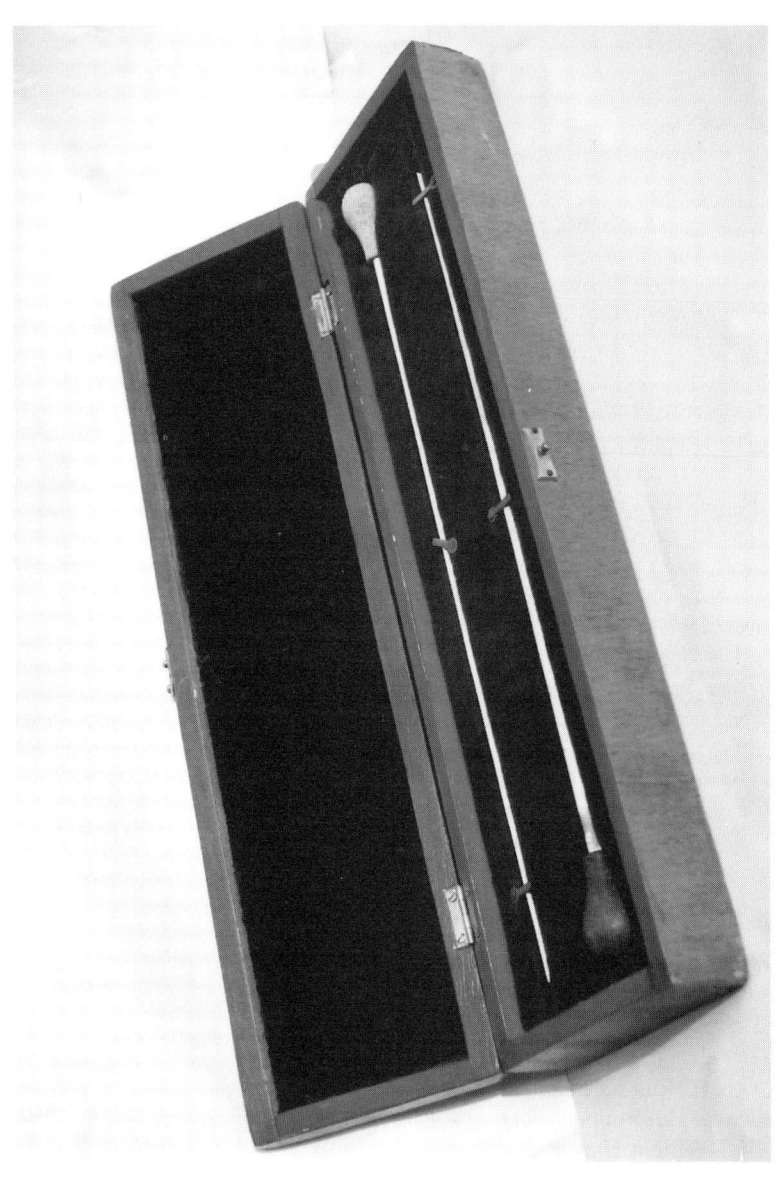

43. Clifford's conducting batons in a case made
For him by Michael Dyer

APPENDIX I
CLIFFORD AND COMPOSITION
An Appreciation by Lionel Pike
(Assistant Organist to Clifford Harker, 1957-59)

Clifford's obituaries were right to maintain that he never made any great claims for his own compositions, for that is quite true: he invariably sent his new works to Dr. Ben Burrows (described by some as the greatest composition teacher in the country) for evaluation and criticism: but that is no more than Vaughan Williams and Holst did with each other's works as long as Holst was alive. Clifford was capable of writing music of great beauty, as witness the little anthem 'Come my way, my truth, my life' with its melting final cadence, or the Nunc Dimittis of his Evening Service in A flat (consciously using a model by Charles Wood); and music of enormous grandeur, as in the D-minor organ prelude on *Iste Confessor* (perhaps his best piece) with its double-pedalled octaves striding like a giant through the texture. But there were also the light miniatures written for pantomimes at the Hippodrome, and often later dug out of the practice-room cupboard during choristers' practices and at Christmas Party times; there was a series of utterly atmospheric pieces of background music produced for Freda Hullcoop's *Guild of Cathedral Players*; and there were countless choir-and-organ arrangements of Christmas Carols, written with mass appeal in mind, for the Carol Concerts that he gave with the Bristol Cathedral Special Choir.

Clifford would teach his pupils composition only as far as the stage where he thought he could take them to no higher level, and he then sent them to Ben Burrows. To that extent he was a modest man; and yet he was one with true insights into the nature and the craft of composition, and he thought deeply about it. He could be quite cutting, if entirely accurate: Rimsky-Korsakoff's *Sheherazade* 'could do with massive cutting', he told me: I doubted it, and it was only years later that I realized that he was right. On the other hand he said with absolute accuracy (and a deep knowledge of the scores) 'Elgar's music always works' and Vaughan Williams's is 'utterly practical'. He dropped *Harris in A* from the Cathedral services because 'Old Doc H [William Harris's nickname] can't get away from the tonic'; and yet he loved the same composer's *Faire is the heaven*. Well after he had retired I asked him if he knew 'Doc H's other double-choir piece in D flat, *Bring us, O Lord God*: as he didn't, I sent him a copy, and he replied on a postcard, with that characteristic big writing, 'It doesn't have the magic of 'In full enjoyment of felicity', and here - on a hand drawn stave - he quoted the treble parts of *Faire is the heaven* at the setting of those words, adding 'I quote from memory'. When he first conducted *The Apostles* and was learning the full score he asked me with great excitement how I would orchestrate the plainsong *O sacrum convivium* which we both only knew from the vocal score. I said I would use the cellos, and (if I remember rightly) he thought the horn, but what thrilled him was the mixture of orchestral sounds that Elgar actually uses ('you wouldn't think it would work; but it does!). His admiration for Wagner's *The Ring* was great, but he found the repetitions irksome; and yet I well remember a wonderful improvisation before Evensong one day when he had just seen *Die Walküre*, and in his own playing and imagination he expressed his great love for the passion of Wagner's music by meditating on Wotan's Farewell to Brünnhilde.

There was a limit to Clifford's tolerance of contemporary music, and he hated anything that, as he put it, 'strives after effect'. He firmly believed in the old values of technical expertize in harmony and counterpoint: we were once on the same little cruise ship on the Rhine (a story in itself...), and he discovered that I was reading Gedalge's *Treatise on the Fugue* in idle moments on deck; he was thrilled to think that people still believed in 'those old values'. And yet, when I was his assistant organist and was providing background music for The Guild of Cathedral Players' production of T.S.Eliot's *Murder in the Cathedral*, he was keen that I should illustrate the murder of Thomas with suitably dramatic music. He would never have written this down: but what he told me to do was to set up the full organ (including the big tuba and the pedal reeds), hold down the bottom three pedal notes together, and place my fists in clusters on the keyboard, going up the Great manual so that there were four thunderous smashes, one for a sword-stroke from each of the knights. I could not see the effect, but I'm told it was shattering and terrifying: and as we now know, such devices (in the 1950s) were well ahead of their time!

May all the trumpets sound for him on the other side.

APPENDIX II
Table of Major Works Performed

Composer	Title	Bristol Cathedral Special Choir (1954-83)	Bristol Choral Society (1960-89)	Bath Choral Society (1963-88)
Bach	St John Passion	1968, 1974, 1983		1985
	St Matthew Passion	1956, 1959, 1962, 1965 1971, 1977, 1980	1966, 1976	
	Mass in B minor	1957, 1964 (with Br.C.S.) 1975, 1979 (with Br.C.S.)	1960, 1964, 1973, 1979	1975
	Wachet Auf (Sleepers wake)			
	Magnificat	1954		1969
	Christmas Oratorio	1965		
Beethoven	Missa Solemnis (Mass in D)	1978	1975, 1980, 1985	
	Choral Fantasia		1965, 1974	1971
	Symphony No.9 (Choral)		1988	
Berlioz	Damnation of Faust		1980	
	Grand Messe des Morts (Requiem)		1962, 1964, 1983 1977, 1982	
	Te Deum	1970, 1973	1975, 1988	
Bliss	Pastoral			1978, 1980
Borodin	Choral Dances from 'Prince Igor'		1963, 1973	1964
Brahms	Song of Destiny	1968	1975, 1980	1968, 1977, 1987
	German Requiem	1954, 1960,	1961, 1968, 1979	1971, 1977, 1987

Brahms German Requiem (Contd.)	1971 (with Bath C.S.) 1982		
Alto Rhapsody	1961, 1966, 1972		
Britten Spring Symphony		1982	
Bruckner Te Deum	1960, 1969		1969
Mass in E	1964		
Psalm 150	1972	1981	
Great Mass in F minor	1976		
Coleridge-Taylor Hiawatha's Wedding Feast		1965	
Delius Songs of Farewell		1971, 1984	
Duruflé Requiem	1966, 1976	1968, 1970, 1983	1983
Dvorak Stabat Mater	1955, 1963, 1977		1970, 1981
Te Deum	1957		
Dyer, Michael Te Deum	1973		
Dyson The Canterbury Pilgrims			1963
Elgar Dream of Gerontius	1955, 1962, 1971, 1972(with Br. C.S.-NFMS Conf) 1978, 1983 (last concert)	1966, 1972, 1981 1987	1967, 1974, 1984
The Kingdom	1957, 1967, 1976	1961, 1972, 1984	1973, 1979, 1988
The Apostles	!974, 1980	1976	
The Music Makers	1975	1960, 1972, 1979, 1984, 1989	1974
Te Deum and Benedictus		1986	1987
Caractacus		1977	
Fauré Requiem	1965, 1972		1968, 1982
German Merrie England	1962, 1969(Colston Hall) 1975(with Bath C.S.)	1969	1975(with Sp. Choir)

Composer	Work	Performance years
Gilbert & Sullivan	Various extracts from Operas	1965, 1973 (with Bath C.S. in Colston Hall) 1989	1970, 1973 (with Sp. Choir)
Handel	Messiah	1963 (Cathedral Restoration Appeal)	Annual performances
	Israel in Egypt		1985
	Acis and Galatea	1981	1967, 1980
	Samson	1966	1969, 1987	1970, 1983
	Zadok the Priest	1966	1970, 1983	1968, 1973, 1982
	Solomon			
	The King Shall Rejoice			1968, 1988
	Thy hand be strengthened			1988
	Te Deum			1984
Haydn	Mass in C (Paukenmesse)	1982		1979
	Imperial Mass	1957		
	Creation	1960, 1969		1966, 1977, 1982
	Theresa Mass	1963	1982	1974
	Mass in B flat	1966		
	Nelson Mass	1970		
	The Seasons		1966 (excerpts)	1971, 1984
Hewitt-Jones, Tony	Sea Poems			1964, 1986 (Spring only)
Holst	Hymn of Jesus	1963, 1975	1968, 1984	1978
Kodaly	Te Deum	1961	1968	
	Psalmus Hungaricus	1967, 1982	1972	1980
	Budavari Te Deum	1979		1973
Kodaly	Missa Brevis		1972	
Mendelssohn	Elijah	1964, 1966 (with Bath C.S.) 1971, 1976 (with B.Sp.Ch.) 1966 (with B.Sp.Ch.) 1976 (with Br.Ch.S.)	1985	1975, 1986

Mendelssohn	Hymn of Praise	1971, 1987
Mozart	Ave verum corpus	1957
	Mass in C minor	1959
	Requiem	1961, 1972 1962, 1969
	Coronation Mass	1967 1978
Offenbach	Tales of Hoffmann (Concert version)	1967, 1971, 1982
Orff	Carmina Burana	1975, 1981, 1986 1965
Parry	Blest Pair of Sirens	1954, 1963 1969, 1978
	I was glad	1970 1972, 1983, 1988 1969, 1973
Poulenc	Gloria	1982, 1986 1972
Puccini	Messa di Gloria	1988 1968, 1978, 1983
Rossini	Petite Messe Solenelle	1957, 1979 1971, 1973, 1984
Schmitt	Psalm 47	1988
Schubert	Mass in A flat	1970 1980
Stanford	Songs of the Fleet	1963, 1983 1986
	Songs of the Sea	1965
Stravinsky Symphony of Psalms		1969, 1974 1973
Tippett	Child of our Time	1965 1966
Vaughan Williams	Sancta Civitas	1969
	Lord, Thou hast been our refuge	1954 1979
	Five Mystical Songs	1972 1976
		1963, 1967, 1980, 1964, 1976, 1985
		1981 (Swansea)

Vaughan Williams		
	Dona Nobis Pacem	1957, 1957(at NFMS Conf)1973
		1981
	Mass in C minor	1962 1974

Vaughan Williams
Benedicite	1967, 1982	
A Sea Symphony		1966, 1976, 1985
Five Tudor Portraits		1967
Mass in G minor		1976

Verdi
Requiem	1956, 1961, 1968(2)(with Bath C.S.) 1973, 1979	1964, 1968(with B.Sp.Ch.) 1976, 1982
Te Deum	1964	1964, 1975, 1987
Four Sacred Pieces	1968	1974, 1979
Aida		1963, 1970, 1978, 1986
Stabat Mater		1961

Vivaldi
Gloria	1965

Wagner
The Flying Dutchman	1967

Walton
Belshazzar's Feast	1966, 1970, 1978
Coronation Te Deum	1969, 1978, 1986

Warren
Continuing Cities	1989

Williamson Mass of Christ the King — 1980, 1981(Swansea)

Orchestral and other Items in Choral Concerts

Arnold
English Dances		1963, 1982
Ov. Tam O'Shanter		1965, 1986

Bach
Passacaglia & Fugue in C minor		1988
Suite in B minor		1978
Brandenberg Concerto No. 3	1965	
Suite No. 3 in D		1962

Bach	Aria for Strings and Organ			1971
Bach/Walton	Suite: The Wise Virgins			1973
Beethoven	Overture Leonora		1965	
	Piano Concerto No. 5		1965	
Brahms	Variations on St. Anthony Chorale		1961	1966
	Academic Festival Overture		1966, 1988	
Dohnanyi	Variations on a Nursery Song		1971	
Elgar	Serenade for Strings	1967	1969, 1980, 1981	1984
	Sursum Corda	1979	1968	1980
	Sea Pictures		1968	1983
	Overture: Cockaigne		1977, 1982	
	Enigma Variations		1963	
Franck	Symphonic Variations for Piano and Orchestra		1968, 1983	
Grieg	Holberg Suite	1972		
Handel	Organ Concerto No. 2 in B flat		1985	
	Organ Concerto No. 4 in F		1970	1969
	Water Music			1968
	Concero Grosso No.12 in B minor			1974, 1988
Handel	Organ Concerto No.13			1988
Haydn	Symphony No. 88	1970		
	Symphony No. 104	1982	1975	
	Symphony No. 1 in G			1965, 1971
	Symphony No. 97			1968
	Military Symphony			1974
Holst	St. Paul's Suite	1975	1954	1978
Mendelssohn	Symphony No. 2	1973, 1981		

Mozart	Eine Kleine Nachtmusik		1974, 1980
	Exsultate Jubilate	1964	
	Symphony No. 39 in E flat		1986
	Symphony No. 40	1971	1964
	Coronation Piano Concerto		1973 (piano solo C.H.)
Offenbach	Overture 'La Belle Helene'		1972
Poulenc	Organ Concerto	1968	1974
Ravel	Pavane		1970
Schubert	Symphony in B minor 'The Unfinished'	1964, 1971	1968, 1971, 1978
	Music from Rosamunde		1973
Vaughan Williams	Fantasia on a Theme by Thomas Tallis	1969	
	Overture 'The Wasps'		1986
	Polka & Fugue from 'Schwanda the Bagpiper'		1973
Weinberger			1967

ACKNOWLEDGEMENTS

To write just a list of names by way of acknowledgement seemed to me to be a rather soulless way to express my gratitude to everyone who had contributed to this volume.

Clifford's influence upon people was always positive; he was probably quite unaware of how much his own ethos was affecting those he worked with. At his retirement dinner, after receiving many ovations, he replied "I really had no idea I was such a splendid chap". It was quite true – he just passed on musical skills and enthusiasm, and got on with what he had to do, with those with whom he worked and played, without any consideration of himself. He expected loyalty, certainly, but desiring a slavish devotion was not part of his make-up, and he did not even consider receiving any return for his labours, save people's own success.

Therefore, the fact that so many of Clifford's friends have been more than generous to me in supplying their opinions, memoirs, and facts about his life, the very least I can do is to make proper record of thanks to those to whom I am greatly indebted, for with these memories the book is infinitely more replete.

I wish, then, to record my own deep thanks to everyone who has given me details for the book – however brief – either by letter, conversation, telephone call, or sight of precious photographs and documents; and I sincerely hope that this volume will not only be a worthy record of Clifford Harker's life, but also stand as a true statement of his greatness.

During the writing of the book I have tried to be meticulous in accuracy and in making note of each person's contribution – great or small. If I have missed naming anyone it has not been intentional and I crave pardon for the omission, hoping that they will recognise their contribution within the pages as the story unfolds, appreciating the enormity of the undertaking.

First, then, my unbounded thanks must go to my dear husband, **John Hilton**, without whose help I should still be floundering at the typewriter! He shared my enthusiasm from the very first and kept a clear path to enable me to research and write. In addition, he has made his own contribution with memories, suggestions and, most of all, he has spent just as many hours as I on the transfer of my typing to the computer, eventually assembling the text into book form ready for the printer. It has been a great joint adventure – and tremendous hard work – but at the same time exciting and rewarding.

Two other people deserving special thanks are **John Jenkins** (chorister 1965-70, Head Chorister 1970) and **Gerry Nichols** (chorister 1959-62, Head Chorister 1961). John provided vital photographs and memorabilia belonging to Clifford, also giving his blessing and encouraging advice. Gerry has given much sound advice in addition to undertaking considerable research in Special Choir archives, photographic assistance, and has given a great deal of practical help.

My son, **Christopher Hilton**, has given valuable technical advice on extending our computer dexterity, as well as supplying mountains of scrap paper!

To my friend, **Margaret Humphreys**, I extend my gratitude for careful proof reading of the text.

I now wish to express my profound gratitude to the following contributors:

Mr. Harry Hoult, of Newcastle, a friend and Cathedral Choir member from Clifford's Newcastle Cathedral days, for his research, photograph, and memories of Newcastle; and to **Mr. Bill Stafford**, also of Newcastle Cathedral Choir. **Mr. John Garratt**, of Wigston, Leicester, for information on Dr. Ben Burrows and celebrated organists; **Rev. Canon Edwin Morris** of Rugby, a pupil of the school in Rugby where Clifford taught; **Mr. Henry Palmer**, (now of Milverton, near Taunton) whose hotel in Clifton was 'home' to Clifford for many years; **Robert Grimley, Dean of Bristol**, for helpful suggestions; and the **Royal College of Music** and the **Royal College of Organists** for details of Clifford's awards.

John Bennett, of Northampton, Clifford's friend throughout the war years and afterwards, who supplied personal memories.

Ted Thompson, of Clevedon, Somerset, for photographs and information on wartime Middle East.

Margaret Chivers, of Thorncombe, near Chard, Somerset, for obtaining 'Cathedral on the Nile' which gave so much interesting historical detail.

Former Choristers:
Lionel Pike (1950-55), Music Department, Organist, and Director of the Chapel Choir, Royal Holloway, University of London, chorister and organ assistant to Clifford, for his memories and notes on Clifford's composition. (Appendix I)
Michael Doswell (1945-49, Head Chorister 1949) of Mitford, near Morpeth, Northumberland. Head Chorister when Clifford arrived at Bristol Cathedral, Clifford's first pupil assistant; became music teacher and conductor of orchestral and choral music.
Geoffrey Hudd (1952-56), of Bath, Somerset; continued with musical interests, becoming organist and choirmaster at his local church; for many interesting and worthwhile comments.
Christopher Chivers (1977- , becoming Head Chorister); became Canon Precentor at the Cathedral Church of St. George the Martyr, Cape Town, South Africa; thanks for his memories and deep appreciation of Clifford's character.
Stephen Parsons (1962-7 Head Chorister 1966); of Backwell, Bristol. Thanks for personal memories and for details of the Bristol Cathedral Old Choristers' Association (as Secretary) and the Choral Foundation.

Stephen Taylor, (1960-) of Utrecht, Holland; also an organ pupil. Studied music at Oxford and Utrecht. Now lives in Holland enjoying a career as nationwide organ recitalist and teacher of organ.

Robert Peters, (Cathedral School, 1940-45, Guild of Cathedral Players, 1945 until early 1980's) of Whitchurch, Bristol,. Thanks for details of Guild of Cathedral Players.

Michael Pain, 1969-71) of Blackburn, Lancashire, music teacher, and organist of Clitheroe Parish Church since 1989.

David Jewell, of Compton Martin, Somerset, former Headmaster of Bristol Cathedral School and member of the Special Choir. My gratitude for his memories and for his profound insight into Clifford's intrinsic qualities.

Rev. Canon David Isitt, of Cambridge, former Canon Precentor at Bristol during Clifford's period. My thanks for his recollections.

Stephen Foulkes, of Brislington, Bristol, for many years a lay clerk, who has since enjoyed an excellent career as a professional singer (bass) and in much demand. My thanks for his detailed memories.

Marion Parsons, of Glastonbury, Somerset. Thanks for her very helpful account of her period as an organ pupil with Clifford.

Ron Apperley, of Clifton, Bristol, for photographic assistance and information on Bristol Cathedral. Also, thanks to **Desmond Tucker** for detail of wartime Bristol.

Edna Knill, of Filton, Bristol, for help with research and for her personal memories as chorister parent.

Canon J.M. Free, of Merriott, Somerset, former Canon Precentor at Bristol Cathedral. Thanks for personal memories and details of the Cathedral chapter.

Rex Hipple, of Bedminster, Bristol, former Sacristan and Head Verger at Bristol during Clifford's period. My thanks for helping enormously with cassettes and other information which sent me on many adventures of research.

Enid Hunt, of Bristol, for details on Bristol orchestras and the Special Choir; **Kathleen Hillier**, of Sherston, Wiltshire, founder member of the Special Choir, for historical and programme details, and information on Diocesan Festivals, my special thanks; and **Muriel George**, of Henleaze, Bristol, for help with information about the Special Choir and music performed.

Alan McCulloch, of Stoke Bishop, Bristol, former Chairman and long serving member of Bristol Choral Society; **Theresa Knowles**, of Clifton, Bristol; **Cecily McKiernan**, of Clevedon, Somerset; **Ken Parsons**, of Downend, Bristol, for their memories of Bristol Choral Society.

Brenda Forbes, of Bath, former Secretary of Bath Choral Society, **George Reddyhoff**, former Programme Editor; and **Jessica Owen**, Secretary of Bath Choral Society; for their help with details of Bath Choral Society; also **Bath Records Office** for access to the archives of Bath Choral Society.

For details and memories of Clifford's **orchestras**, **John Giddings**, of Stoke Bishop, Bristol, (timpanist) provided much information as well as helping me to contact former orchestral players. **Margaret Wills** (cello) and **John Wills** (Double Bass), of Downend, Bristol; **John Dixon**, (cello) of Redland, Bristol; **David Mason** (solo trumpet) of London; **Stewart McKim** (double bass) of Batheaston, Somerset; **Jim Gowers** (bassoon), of Henbury, Bristol; **Anne Patrick**, of Backwell, Somerset; and **Elizabeth Palmer** (bassoon), of Westbury on Trym, Bristol; my sincere thanks for providing lively and valuable contributions.

Raymond Holland, of Frampton Cotterell, Bristol, helped greatly with historical detail concerning the Madrigal Society; and **Nesta Parsons**, of Downend, Bristol, provided photographs and detail of the Lord Mayor's Chapel and Choir.

Roger Crudge, former Senior Librarian at Bristol Central Library, and Special Choir member, provided advice on access to Clifford's music in the Central Library, and gave personal memories.

University of Bristol and **University of the West of England**, for details of degree ceremonies.

Rev. Canon Frank Dexter (Parish Church of St. George, Jesmond, Newcastle) for much willing help with church and organ details.

Mr. Stanley Davidson, organist of St. Andrew's Parish Church, Newcastle, for information about Clifford's period at that church.

Lesley Wright and the **Dean of St. Nicholas Cathedral Church, Newcastle**, for detail of the Cathedral and its organ.

Johnathan Lane, of Rugby, organist, teacher, writer and composer, my gratitude for information about Rugby Church organ and about Clifford's music; and **Rhona Smith**, Parish Secretary, for photograph and detail of St. Andrew's Parish Church, Rugby.

Walter Galvin,, of Kenn, Clevedon, Somerset, for providing specification of the organ in the Lord Mayor's Chapel.

Robert Payne, of Henleaze, Bristol, thanks for the detail of the Lord Mayor's Chapel choir and further detail of Clifford's compositions.

The Very Rev. A.H. Dammers, former Dean of Bristol Cathedral, for his memories expressed in the funeral oration.

Ronald Bleach, of Redland, Bristol, my thanks for details relating to the Elgar Society and of Clifford's involvement, and for his personal memories.

Raymond Hillman, of Stoke Bishop, Bristol, for much help with details of the Bristol Organists' Association, and of Clifford's involvement.

Alan Canterbury, verger of the Lord Mayor's Chapel, for his willing help with detail of the Chapel, and for his memories.

Photographic Acknowledgements
Book cover: Coloured photograph of floodlit Cathedral.   Photo:P.G. Young
Newcastle Cathedral Choir   by kind permission of Mr. Harry Hoult

Clifford and Bristol Cathedral Choir	photo: Cyril Moorhead
Bristol Choral Society	Photo loaned by Nesta Parsons
Lord Mayor's Chapel Choir	Photo: Bromhead (Bristol) Ltd.
St. George's Church, Jesmond	by kind permission of the vicar and PCC
Newcastle Cathedral organ	Dean and Chapter of Newcastle Cathedral Photo: J.R.L. Smith
St. Andrew's Church, Rugby	photo: the Rector and Wardens
Lord Mayor's Chapel, Bristol	Photo: Gerry Nichols
Clifford at the organ of Bristol Cathedral	Photo: Woodmansterne
Bristol Cathedral organ case and choir	3 photos: Jarrold Publishing
Bristol Cathedral Nave	(Pitkin Pictorials)
Bristol Cathedral rear view and garden	
Bristol Cathedral Eastern Lady Chapel organ	Photo: Stanley R. Nichols
Middle East photographs	Ted Thompson

All other illustrations by kind permission of John Jenkins

Bibliography
Cathedral on the Nile (Arthur Burrell) Pub. Amate Press Ltd. Oxford, in 1984
Rejoice Greatly (George Bowen)   pub. White Tree Books, 1988
Concerning the Bristol Madrigal Society (Hubert Hunt) 1948,   private pub.
The Bristol Madrigal Society (Herbert Byard) 1966,   private pub.
St. Mark's, the Lord Mayor's Chapel, Bristol (Elizabeth Ralph and Henley Evans) 1961, private pub.
St. Mark's the Lord Mayor's Chapel, Bristol (Alan Canterbury) 1998, private pub.